Shoot Your Shot

A Sport-Inspired Guide to Living Your Best Life

VERNON BRUNDAGE JR.

Shoot Your Shot:

A Sport-Inspired Guide to Living Your Best Life

Disclaimer: The advice and strategies contained herein may not be suitable for every situation. This work is sold with the understanding that the Author and Publisher are not engaged in rendering legal, accounting, or other professional services. Further, readers should be aware that the websites referenced in this work may have changed or been removed between when this work was written and when it is read.

First Printing: 2018

ISBN 978-1-719-90038-6

www.vernonbrundage.com

Ordering Information:

U.S. trade bookstores and wholesalers: Please contact Vernon Brundage Jr. via email: Vernon@vernonbrundage.com

This book is dedicated to those who have been with me shootin' in the gym.

You are eternally appreciated.

CONTENTS

OVERTIME

PREGAME

In recent years, the motto 'shoot your shot' has taken on a life of its own. While its' origin is sport-based—i.e., you shoot your shot in basketball, soccer, hockey, etc.—the expression is more frequently being used in society's everyday lingo.

Nowadays, the saying primarily characterizes a person's pursuit of a romantic interest. (One of the most notable examples being Philadelphia 76ers star center Joel Embiid 'shooting his shot' at music icon Rihanna.) We see it in social media posts, hashtags, and statuses. People use it in everyday conversations amongst friends via phone, text, virtual chat, or face to face. Even the highly popular nationally syndicated morning radio show Power 105.1's *The Breakfast Club* had a daily segment called 'Shoot Your Shot.'

Although the pop cultural use of 'shoot your shot' is most often meant to be entertaining and funny, valid questions to ask relating to this axiom are, "What if we applied this 'shoot your shot' mentality to facets of our everyday lives and what kind of impact would it have on our outcomes?" If you really take a second to think about it, the saying's underlying meaning is quite profound.

You see, unless we 'shoot our shot'—whether it is playing sports, pursuing a romantic interest, or striving to accomplish our personal goals—we will never be able to win. We will never be able to live our best lives.

What exactly does 'living your best life' mean? Honestly, it can mean whatever you want it to. Traveling frequently; owning your own business; having a deck or a pool or a big backyard at your house; working in your desired profession; playing varsity, college, or professional sports; buying your dream car; raising a family; being at your desired weight; having your own talk show; writing your own bestselling book. Living your best life is tailored specifically to you. It is doing, being, and having whatever makes you happy.

In a sport like basketball, in order to score a player must shoot. There is no other way for you to score (at least purposely, that is) than to consciously and deliberately shoot the ball. In our lives, in order to get what we want, we must take a similar approach: Do certain things and perform certain tasks that will move us closer towards accomplishing the goals we have set for ourselves. Basically, we have to shoot our shot.

Just as sports in general can be used as a metaphor for life, the saying 'shoot your shot' can serve as a metaphor for pursuing what you want in life.

If you couldn't tell by now, sports (particularly basketball) have had a profound impact on my life. The lessons that I learned from playing, watching, and studying the game of basketball have served as catalysts for my own life progression.

While I value education and know how important it is in regards to literacy and career progression, I have to admit that I've learned many more applicable life lessons from my involvement in sports than I have from most school subjects or historical figures.

Quite frankly, I've learned more about life from watching Michael Jordan will his team to victory while battling the flu or witnessing LeBron James and the Cleveland Cavaliers come back from being down 3-1 in the 2016 NBA Finals to win the championship than I did from taking a chemistry or a social studies course. I identify more with Russell Westbrook than I do with Mark Zuckerberg. And, I am personally more inspired by Kobe Bryant than I am by Reverend Al Sharpton.

No disrespect or undermining intended, but this is my truth and I am pretty sure I am not the only one who feels this way. Which is what prompted me to write this book.

If basketball has helped me become the man I am today, I'm convinced that certain principles from the court and the stories of former and current players as well as personnel can help you, the reader, too. And maybe, just maybe, you will begin to look at sports as more than just recreation and entertainment, but also as a source of motivation, inspiration, and teachable moments.

Shoot Your Shot is a combination of several of my passions and interests: basketball, writing, research, and inspiring others. This is an unconventional approach to the self-help genre, and one that has not been used before in this particular format. It is a major risk, but one thing I have learned (from basketball, of course) is that you miss all of the shots you don't take. I sincerely believe that we are never given an idea unless we have everything we need to see it all the way through.

Although the title of this book is *Shoot Your Shot*, there are so many factors other than shooting in basketball that help lead a team to victory and contribute to success on and off the court. I wanted to explore several of those other components in detail as well to show how they each relate to our lives and how they can help us on our own individual paths.

Shoot Your Shot is universal. Although it may appeal to a younger demographic and to sports fans, it is not age, gender, socioeconomic status, or race specific. Your background and standing are irrelevant. This book is for anyone with an open mind and an overwhelming desire to live his or her best life.

Sports are often referred to as a common thread that brings people together regardless of their age, gender, race, or socioeconomic status. My hope is that this sport-based book inspires you to go after the goals you have set for yourself and motivates you to do what is necessary to realize the life you have always envisioned.

The principles presented in this book align directly with those commonly advocated for in self-help books, Scripture, and motivational speeches. Many of which come directly from those that I have personally read, studied, and listened to on my path towards realizing the life I envisioned for myself. Thus, I am not just pulling these principles out of thin air but rather providing them to you as a result of extensive research, studying, and life experience.

No matter your circumstances, I truly believe you will be able to use the principles and examples in this book to help you on your own journey towards accomplishing the goals you have set for yourself.

With that being said, play the game of life to the absolute fullest. You cannot win if you are timid or reluctant. And you certainly cannot get what you want out of life without shooting your shot. Regardless of how many times you miss, keep shooting until you make the goal. The only way you can possibly win is if you shoot your shot, until your shot goes in. I appreciate you for taking this journey with me. Let's get into it.

-*VB*

FIRST
QUARTER

1

Remove Limitations

There shouldn't be any limitations...it's about talent and the ability to do things. It's not about what your sex is or your race or anything else.
GREGG POPOVICH
5-time NBA champion as a coach, 3-time NBA Coach of the Year, and current head coach of the San Antonio Spurs

For me, basketball was one of the first dispellers of the myth that my background or where I lived dictated the trajectory of my life. As a huge basketball fan growing up in a moderate-to-middle class community located right outside of Philadelphia, Pennsylvania, I saw this collective of extraordinarily-talented and skilled individuals on television from October to June who looked like me, came from similar if not worse backgrounds as I did, doing what they loved to do, and earning a pretty handsome paycheck while doing it.

None of them would be in that position had they believed where they came from, what they lacked growing up, the color of their skin, or their background determined their ability to be successful. They would also not be in the positions they were in had they listened to the words of doubters and naysayers.

Jeremy Lin, Becky Hammon, Violet Palmer, and Giannis Antetokounmpo all have one thing in common: They refused to use their background as an excuse and a limiting factor in the realization of their dreams. As a result, and in their own regard, they each defied odds in the NBA.

Jeremy Lin is the first American of Chinese or Taiwanese descent to play in the NBA. Seeking success as an Asian American in an African-American dominated sport, Lin went undrafted during the 2010 NBA draft despite receiving countless collegiate accolades. Lin as well as other coaches and NBA personnel speculate that him not being drafted was due to his Asian-American heritage.[i]

Early in Lin's career, if he wasn't riding a team's bench then he was bouncing in and out of the league. Due to the uncertainty of his place in the NBA and the fact that he moved around so much, Lin routinely slept on his brother's couch and on the couches of his teammates. However, in 2012 while playing for the New York Knicks and making the most of an opportunity afforded to him due to injuries to key players on the team, Lin rose to international stardom for a brief period of time renowned as "Linsanity." Over a 26-game span, Lin averaged almost 18 points and 8 assists per game. Since then, he has maintained a steady job in the league as a contributing point guard on each team he plays for.

Former WNBA star Becky Hammon broke gender barriers in 2014, becoming the first full-time salaried female coach in the history of the NBA when she accepted a job as an assistant coach on the San Antonio Spurs coaching staff. In 2015, she was elected to serve as the head coach of the Spurs summer league team, becoming the first woman to be a head coach of an NBA summer league team. That same summer, Hammon became the first female head coach to win a summer league as well, after leading the Spurs to the championship. In the spring of 2018, she also became the first woman to interview for a head-coaching job in the NBA.

Violet Palmer also defied odds in the NBA. A former standout collegiate women's basketball player from Compton,

California, Palmer worked her way up the officiating ranks to became the first woman to officiate in the NBA. She is recognized as the first female official in any major professional sport in the United States. In 2006, Palmer became the first woman to officiate an NBA playoff game—a task delegated to only high performing referees—and in 2009, she officiated the NBA Finals, the first woman to do that as well.

And then there's Giannis Antetokounmpo. The son of Nigerian immigrants, Antetokounmpo was born into poverty in Athens, Greece on December 6, 1994. With no citizenship documents from Nigeria or Greece, the family of six dwelled in small two-room apartments, sleeping three-to-four to a bed at times. As a kid, Giannis and his older brother Thanasis would peddle goods on the street in order to make money so that their family could get by.

Encouraged by his father to explore a possible career in basketball, Giannis began playing basketball in 2007. By 2012, he was playing in Greece's second-tier basketball league with his brother. Although the brothers were making more money than they were selling watches, bags, sunglasses and other goods on the street, they weren't making enough to afford multiple pairs of sneakers and often had to share the same pair of sneakers during games.[ii]

In 2013, after attracting the attention of NBA scouts when game footage of him went viral, Giannis made himself eligible for the NBA Draft at the age of 18. The Milwaukee Bucks selected him with the 15th pick in the 2013 NBA Draft. Coming into the league as a tall, skinny, raw talent, Giannis has transformed his body, polished his game, and is now revered as "The Greek Freak." Analysts as well as his peers often herald him as the future of the NBA.

From the 2013-2014 NBA season to the 2017-2018 season, Giannis' output increased from 6.8 points, 4.4 rebounds, and 1.9 assists per game to 26.9 points, 10.0 rebounds, and 4.8 assists per game. He led the Bucks to the NBA playoffs in 2015, 2017 and 2018. He was selected as an NBA All-Star in 2017 and 2018. Prior to his All-Star selections, Giannis signed a $100 million contract with Milwaukee in 2016; in 2017, he become the first foreign-born player to have his very own signature shoe made by Nike. Giannis Antetokounmpo has come a long way from hawking sunglasses and sharing shoes.

When you try to use your race, your gender, your age, or your socioeconomic standing as an excuse for why you are unable to do something, just think of these individuals and those like them who have defied odds to realize their dreams and made a better life for themselves and their families.

In life, we can either be our own greatest ally or our worst enemy. Nothing outside of us has the power to dictate our outcomes. As you think, so shall you be. The thoughts that you have about yourself will eventually manifest themselves in reality.

I am fully aware that our circumstances help to shape us into who we become as individuals. Our upbringing and the experiences we've had teach us valuable lessons and provide us with tremendous insight. However, our experiences and our upbringing do not determine what we can and cannot do in life. Only we do. Only our thoughts, our faith, and our efforts determine the outcomes of our lives. Once you stop looking outside of yourself for answers and start looking inward, then you will be able to start the process of seeing the desired changes occur in your life.

Oftentimes we limit ourselves because we have told ourselves or have been told by teachers, family members, friends, coaches, or loved ones that we will never amount to anything. We've ruled ourselves out of attaining certain things just because we come from a specific geographic area or a particular background. We see ourselves as nothing more than a product of the environments in which we were raised.

Because we were born into a low-income family or because we are the first in our family to go to college or because we did not perform the best in school or because we haven't received adequate guidance or because we did not go to the top schools, we've convinced ourselves that we will never be able to advance in life. We make excuses, maybe out of fear or to avoid accountability, that only stunt our ability to grow. Hence, we've surrendered to our circumstances. We've ruled ourselves out of attaining greatness before even making an attempt to tap into the unbounded potential within us.

All because we've believed the lies we've been telling ourselves for so long and the story that someone else has attempted to write for us.

Think about it. Growing up, you never placed limitations on yourself until someone else did. You thought you could do and be anything, didn't you? You had huge dreams of becoming a doctor, an artist, a pilot, a lawyer, a business-person, a professional athlete, a dentist, and a veterinarian, among countless other professions. But as soon as some-one—a teacher, guardian, friend, sibling, classmate, etc.—told you that you couldn't do this or you couldn't do that, that was the point when you began to doubt yourself, your capabilities, and your dreams.

For example, when I was a kid, I loved to draw. I mean LOVED it. If I wasn't in my own imaginary world playing with my Ninja Turtles, Power Rangers, or WWF action figures, I was drawing. But then in elementary school one of my art teachers told me that my drawings weren't good and even accused me of tracing a drawing from a book, even though you could clearly see it was drawn by hand.

As a 9-year old little boy, I was crushed and mentally scarred. I doubted myself along with my artwork and trusted the subjective opinion of someone else more than I believed in the capabilities I possessed within me. So, I gave up drawing for good. I unfairly and erroneously limited myself.

As I grew older and matured, I was taught a valuable lesson: When you limit yourself, you ultimately limit what God is able to do in your life. Everything surely happens for a reason, but who knows which way my life would have went had I believed in myself more than the opinion of someone else. Nowadays, no one can tell me anything about what I can and cannot do. I'm not willing to limit what God can do in my life nor block my blessings based on someone else's opinion. You shouldn't be either.

Imagine if Michael Jordan believed his coaches were right to cut him from the varsity basketball team in his sophomore year of high school. We may have never witnessed arguably the greatest basketball player to ever wear an NBA uniform.

We would've missed out on seeing MJ soar from the free throw line, lead the Bulls to six NBA titles, hit the game winning shot in Game 6 of the 1998 NBA Finals, or last, but certainly not least, see him and the rest of the *Looney Tunes* bunch defeat the MonStars in *Space Jam*. (Say what you want about the movie but *Space Jam* is a classic and a relic of my childhood).

Michael Jordan is just one example, but just think about the people (athletes and non-athletes) who you admire or look up to. What if these impactful individuals gave up on their dreams or their passions based on the opinions and disapproval of others? They would have never reached their full potential, would not have become the individuals they always aspired to be, nor would they be the people who inspire you to do more with your life.

Don't downgrade your dreams to fit someone else's reality. What you accomplish in life is a direct result of your actions, your thoughts, and your perception of yourself. You are within arm's reach of attaining the life you want to live. However, you have to be willing to extend beyond the limitations you have placed on yourself and the limitations others have placed on you. You, and only you, are the sole decision maker in what your story is going to be. When you change how you view yourself, you will then be able to change the course of your life.

Take some time for reflection. Visualize the life experience you want for yourself in profound detail. Write down your goals and aspirations. Print out pictures of what you want and put them on a vision board for you to reflect on daily. Develop affirmations, or positive statements, about yourself and recite them every day. See yourself in your desired state of dwelling and believe that it is possible to attain it.

Sometimes we get in our own way, especially when we believe we do not have the power to change our conditions. This error in thinking must be eliminated if you are to live your best life. Make the commitment to work for what it is that you want in order to make the new and improved story that you tell yourself, and the one you replay over and over in your head, a reality.

Another action that is important to carry out while pursuing your best life is guarding your speech. Proverbs 18:21 (NIV) states, "The tongue has the power of life and death." Be mindful to never speak of yourself in a negative or discouraging way. Only speak life into yourself and about how you are advancing on your way to living your best life. At some point, you are going to have to make the choice between the life you've grown accustomed to and the life you want to live. Truly believe without a shadow of a doubt that what you want can and will come to fruition. See yourself where you want to be and hold tightly onto to that vision with everything you've got.

Your age, race, gender, background, or geographic area has nothing to do with what you can or cannot accomplish. Only your commitment, the work you put in, an unrelenting faith, and the story you tell yourself about yourself matter.

You may have this preconceived notion that living an abundant life is only possible for those who satisfy certain prerequisites (i.e., coming from a wealthy family, going to the best schools, living in a particular area code, etc.). If this were the case then only a select number of people, from a certain area, with a particular background, and specific qualifications would be living the lives they've envisioned for themselves. We know that is not true because we have witnessed otherwise in sports, business, music, and many other industries.

There are multitudes of individuals from a variety of different backgrounds who are making an impact on the world and who are doing what they love to do. You can do the same. Don't let your history, a false narrative, or unfavorable circumstances dictate your outcomes.

Take control over your life. Dispel the myth that your background determines your outcomes. Believe in yourself even when others don't believe in you. Cease living your life according to the rules that someone else said you must abide by because of his or her inability to see *their* own potential for greatness. Because honestly, that's what it really comes down to when others try to limit you. If someone cannot or refuses to recognize the greatness they possess within themselves, what makes you think he or she will see the greatness within you? They're not going to.

You may not have the typical background for a particular career or endeavor, but don't let that be what stops you from pursuing what it is that you want in life. Go get it if that's what you really want. You are fully capable of attaining any and everything you could possibly dream of irrespective of where you come from, your family history, or even your past actions.

Regardless of statistics.

Regardless of the lies you've been telling yourself for so long.

Regardless of the misguided and ill-informed opinions of others.

Regardless of what you have or have not done up to this point in your life.

You are able to do anything you set your mind to.

You living your best life starts with separating yourself from anything that does not help you become better or attain more. Changing the rules on what controls you, ultimately changes the rules on what you are able to control. Break free from those imaginary shackles called limitations that you've placed on your potential so long ago. Get out of your own way so you can get to where you want to go.

2

Take Responsibility For Your Own Outcomes

Accountability is essential to personal growth as well as team growth. How can you improve if you are never wrong? If you don't admit a mistake and take accountability for it, you're bound to make the same one again.

PAT SUMMITT

8-time NCAA women's basketball champion as a coach, 7-time NCAA Coach of the Year, 2nd most career wins in NCAA Division I history, and the Naismith Coach of the 20th Century

After virtually every NBA game, media personnel interview the coaches and players from both the winning and the losing teams. When coaches or players from the losing team are interviewed, more often than not, they will attribute the loss to missteps made by the team as a whole, or proceed to place the full responsibility of the loss on themselves.

Nevertheless, in rare instances we see players and coaches place the blame for a loss on bad calls made by the referees, an opposing player, their teammates, the fans, the court, the arena, the rim, or the ball. Anybody or anything other than where the responsibility actually falls upon—themselves. As expected, that team usually does not accomplish their goal of winning a championship (or even make the playoffs for that matter) because they fail to take responsibility for their circumstances.

Nothing can ever be changed in your life unless responsibility is assigned to the appropriate party. And the appropriate party in every instance is, and always will be, YOU. You are currently in this stage of life because of you, and only you. Some of us refuse to accept this. We've convinced ourselves that it is everyone and everything else's fault for our current standing in life.

In order to progress in life and get out of the current circumstances you may find yourself in, you have to take responsibility for everything that has happened up to this point in your life. Own up to your own stuff. The failed relationships. The struggling business. Your inability to get a job or a promotion. Not meeting your weight loss or fitness goals. Not making the team. Not graduating from high school or college. Not going on that dream trip. In every situation that you find yourself in, you are always the common denominator. Therefore, you, and only you, have the power to transform the outcomes in your life.

When you accept that you are the master of your own fate, you will *then* be able to make the necessary changes that will propel your life to the next level. But first, you have to get out of your own way.

Getting out of your own way not only means removing limitations and getting out of a toxic headspace as we discussed in the previous section. It also means accepting responsibility for everything that has happened up to this point and everything that is currently going on in your life. When you place the blame for your circumstances on everyone and everything else, you are basically saying you have no control over anything that happens in your life. Even though this particular life experience is specific to you.

Too often, we place the blame on outside factors for our own lack of attaining certain things. Or make excuses for why things don't go the way we want them to.

"If my job paid me more, I could afford the lifestyle I want."

"If I didn't have all these kids and family members to take care then I'd have the time to follow my dreams."

"No jobs will hire me because 'the man' is holding me down."

"My parents didn't prepare me for school or help with my homework so that's why I'm failing out."

"My body's metabolism isn't the same as it was when I was younger so it's impossible to get this weight off of me."

"He/she treats me terribly and isn't willing to change, that's why the relationship isn't working."

Yada. Yada. Yada.

Excuse after excuse after excuse.

We're all guilty. No one is exempt. Countless times, we've used excuses to some extent to avoid responsibility for our outcomes.

Taking the lines directly from the poem *Excuses* (author unknown), "Excuses are tools of incompetence used to build bridges to nowhere and monuments of nothingness, and those who use them seldom specialize in anything else."

If you don't want to put in the necessary work to change your circumstances, making illegitimate excuses is probably the best thing you could ever do. Making an excuse and misplacing blame are active ways of avoiding taking responsibility and holding yourself accountable. Excuses spare you from really evaluating yourself and your approach to a specific situation. They also hinder growth and block you from your potential. Be prepared to remain right where you are because you cannot progress in life by continually making excuses or placing unnecessary blame on others.

You think that just because I'm writing this, I'm exempt? *Not at all.* In high school, I finally began coming into my own as a basketball player. However, I thought I deserved more recruiting interest than I was generating. At the end of my senior season, I didn't receive one scholarship offer to play collegiately. And so, my very own blame game commenced.

I mean it couldn't have been me. No, I did *everything* in my power to earn an athletic scholarship. So it *had* to be someone (if not everybody) else's fault.

I blamed my coaches for not advocating on my behalf and for not doing enough to market me to college basketball programs.

I blamed my father for not sending me to the top camps or signing me up for AAU teams.

I blamed a former teammate for transferring to another school because when he left, college coaches stopped coming to our games.

I even blamed my mother for being 5'3 because if she was just a couple inches taller I would've been at least

6'0 and, oh without a doubt, I would be getting recruited by all the top basketball programs in the nation. Scratch that, I may have even gone straight from high school to the NBA had she been taller. (I am not making this up. This was really my thought process.)

I made excuses and placed unwarranted blame on others because, in all actuality, I knew deep down that I really didn't do everything in my power to play basketball at the next level.

Truth be told, I was good, but I wasn't *that* good. I didn't work on my game like I should have—until it was too late. I didn't save money or raise funds in order to sponsor *my own way* to camps, into leagues, or onto an AAU team. I didn't talk to my coach or my athletic director regularly in order to map out an approach to get coaches to come to my high school games and see me play. I didn't reach out to coaching staffs personally or attempt to build a good rapport with them.

I can go on and on with a laundry list of things I didn't do but point blank, I just didn't handle my business like I was supposed to. As opposed to being painfully truthful and honest with myself at the time, I looked for external entities to confront and blame. And because I opted to place blame elsewhere instead of doing what was necessary on my own, I found myself in the predicament that I was in: not being recruited to play basketball collegiately. I was the sole person responsible for my circumstances, no matter how much I tried to avoid this reality.

The moment you accept responsibility for your current standing, you are then in a position to fully take charge of your life and change the things that you view as unfavorable. Do what is necessary in order to achieve your goals, without assigning blame to external entities when things don't go your way.

You are in full control of your life. Get rid of excuses. Stop playing the blame game. Stop playing the victim. Take 100% responsibility for your life. Only then will you be able to achieve the results that you desire.

3

Put In The Work And
Prepare Adequately

*I'm going to be a success at whatever I choose because
of my preparation. By the time the game starts, the
outcome has been decided. I never think about having a
bad game because I am prepared.*
DAVID ROBINSON
*2-time NBA champion, 10-time NBA All-Star, 1995 NBA MVP,
and a 2009 Naismith Basketball Hall of Fame inductee*

Proper planning and preparation prevents piss poor performance. This military adage, known as the Seven Ps, clearly
communicates that your performance is based on prior planning and preparation. If you fail to plan (or prepare) then you
plan (or prepare) to fail. The work you put in and the critical
steps you take prior to completing your objective dictate
whether you will be successful or unsuccessful.

The greatest basketball players in the world understand that in order to perform effectively on the court, they must put in all the unseen hours and underappreciated work before even stepping foot onto the court for a regulation NBA game. Studying film, lifting weights, running drills, putting up shots, eating right. This is the work that is necessary if they want to take their games to the next level and separate themselves from their competitors. These actions provide them with a competitive advantage because everybody is not willing to put in the time and make the necessary sacrifices in order to be the best. Others would rather be in the club, scrolling through social media timelines, and hanging with friends as opposed to working on themselves and their craft.

In whatever endeavor you are pursuing, preparation is the key if you want to have longstanding success. In order to be successful at anything in life, you must prepare adequately. You must be willing to put in the work and go that extra mile even when you don't feel like it. The degree to which you prepare is always on full display in your performance and the results of your endeavors. You can always tell how a person prepared by observing their outcomes.

The grade you get on an exam. Whether you passed a test to earn a certification. Whether you made the team.

Whether you got the job offer. Whether you met your fitness goals. Whether you received the business grant. Your results are reflections of the degree to which you prepared and the amount of work you put in prior to completing a particular task. Essentially, the end product always has a direct correlation with your degree of preparation. How you prepare is how you perform.

An NBA regular season is generally stretched out across an 8-month period, leaving about 4 months for players to prepare and improve their game in the offseason. The main goal for a player in the offseason is (or at least should be) to come back better than they were the previous season in order to, first off, keep their job, but to also improve the likelihood of earning more playing time, getting a contract extension or a max contract offer, becoming a key or star player, making the all-star team, and ultimately, helping their team win a championship.

The league is comprised of about 400 players. One would think every single one of them would have an incentive to work extremely hard in order to retain their jobs due to the high turnover in the league in addition to having a desire to accomplish the goals listed above, right? Wrong. Some players are content with just making a roster, collecting a hefty paycheck, and enjoying the perks of being a professional athlete for a few years.

Do they possess talent? Of course. But the issue is not their talent, it is their unwillingness to go the extra mile to standout and set themselves apart from the rest of their peers.

There is a reason why players in the league have the distinction of being superstars, starters, regular rotation players, or benchwarmers. Yes, natural ability has something to do with it but the title a player garners, the role they play on a team, and the amount of playing time they get is primarily due to the fact that some of them are willing to put in more work and prepare more than others.

You know how the saying goes: *Hard work beats talent when talent doesn't work hard.*

That is exactly why you see top-rated players coming out of high school or college flop in the NBA and athletes who flew under-the-radar end up becoming successful. Some relied solely on their natural abilities and got complacent thinking that their talent would carry them for the entirety of their careers while others prepared adequately and consistently worked at their craft.

Ask yourself, do you want to be like one of those complacent players and just scrape by in your life? Or do you want to be like those players who are willing to do the necessary work that elevates them above the rest of the field? I hope you choose to be the latter and put in the required effort to get to where you want to be.

I often read and watch content that profiles the players I admire in the NBA and highlights their work ethic.

While in college, Stephen Curry was in the gym at 6am working out and would have multiple shooting sessions throughout the day to improve his jump shot. Before games, he also has intense dribbling sessions that translate to effective ball handling during games.

Kawhi Leonard worked on his game so much while playing for the San Antonio Spurs that he sometimes had to be escorted off the court after practice by his coaching staff as a means to prevent exhaustion and injury.

LeBron James is regularly the first of his teammates to arrive at practice and the last one to leave, which has aided him in being considered one of the greatest all-around basketball players of all time.

Russell Westbrook is known for watching hours and hours of film so he can identify a competitive advantage on the court and improve his play.

Dirk Nowitzki worked tirelessly on his shooting mechanics and his footwork in order to master his patented step-back jump shot that has made him one of the most dominant scorers in NBA history.

Each one of these examples shows a common theme of preparing adequately and maintaining a commitment to one's craft. This is the behavior that keeps them at the top of their games and sets them apart from their peers in the league.

So in your own life, how can you incorporate their approach to the game into your every day life? First, start small. Little by little, a little becomes a lot. All the seemingly diminutive and insignificant steps you carry out while pursuing your goals are actually critical to the attainment of that which you desire. How you do the small things, will ultimately be how you do the big things. If you put in a half way effort when you prepare, that half way effort will be what you put out when it's time for you to perform.

In the words of Joel Embiid and Philadelphia 76ers fans, "Trust the process." Every assertive action you carry out up until you accomplish your goal is significant and inches you closer and closer to your desired end result.

Progress is a process. Success is only a consequence of the decisions you have made and the actions you have carried out regardless of how you feel or what you're going through. Being lazy has never resulted in favorable outcomes. Do what you need to do even when you don't feel like doing it in order to become the person you desire to become. Be patient. Be persistent. There are no quick fixes to long-standing success.

The extra time that was put into practicing, watching film, working on their bodies and on their games prepared players like Curry, Nowitzki, James, Leonard, and Westbrook for the key moments that have defined their careers. They had no idea if or when those moments would come, but they were prepared nonetheless and have shown up more often than not. Because when you stay ready, you never have to get ready.

It is more beneficial to be prepared for an opportunity and for one not to present itself, than for an opportunity to present itself and not be prepared for it. If you consistently do the little things, you will be prepared for your moment. Take pride in your work no matter how menial the task may appear.

Ray Allen (also known as Jesus Shuttlesworth for his timeless role in *He Got Game*) had one of the most beautiful, accurate, and effective jump shots in the history of the NBA. It was like poetry-in-motion watching him shoot the basketball.

Allen once said the following: "When people say God blessed me with a beautiful jump shot, it really pisses me off. I tell those people, 'Don't undermine the work I've put in every day.' Not some days. Every day. Ask anyone who has been on a team with me who shoots the most…the answer is me—not because it's a competition, but because that's how I prepare."

Ray Allen just so happens to be the all-time leader in three-point shots made and a 2018 Naismith Basketball Hall of Fame inductee. Now, I would hope that Jesus (I mean Ray) recognizes that he has been blessed with athletic abilities far greater than the common person. At the same time, I understand where he is coming from. He was emphasizing the point that he worked tirelessly at his craft and got to where he was because of the degree to which he practiced and prepared. Ray Allen is a living embodiment of the old adage, "Practice makes perfect."

Practice? We're talking about practice? *In my best Allen Iverson voice*

(Sorry it was too tempting not to write that but yes, we are talking about practice.)

Whatever it is that you desire to accomplish in life requires certain monotonous processes that must be carried out on a regular basis. Ball players practice the same shots over and over again at game speed whether it's a bank shot, fade-a-way, step back jumper or reverse lay-up and at certain spots on the court in order to increase the probability of making those types of shots during games. The only way for you to improve in a certain area and increase your own likelihood of success is to continue to do the same thing repetitively until you reach the level that you desire to be at.

Whatever you want to be, whatever you want to do, whatever you want to accomplish, there are going to be certain actions that you must carry out in a repetitive and consistent manner. Do not just go through the motions. Put forth your best effort every time you perform a task that corresponds to your objective.

The necessity for you to put in the work and properly prepare also requires making sacrifices if you want to accomplish anything in life. There is an opportunity cost—or a tradeoff—associated with every decision you make. That is, you must give up one thing (or several things) in order for you to acquire or achieve something else.

If you want to reach your goal weight, you're going to have to give up the chips, the chocolate, and the cookies.

If you want to start your own business, you're going to have to spend some Friday or Saturday nights in the library doing research and drawing up a business plan instead of being in the club or in front of the television.

If you want to earn your degree, you're going to have to sacrifice some sleep and time with friends in order to devote that extra time to doing homework and studying for exams.

As difficult as it may be, it is necessary to have the discipline and the willingness to push aside anything that serves as an impediment to your progress in accomplishing your goal. That's the cost of being successful at any feat.

In order to establish themselves as the elite athletes that they are, NBA players have had to sacrifice time with family and friends and have gone without participating in extracurricular activities to instead spend time in the weight room, on the court, and in the film room in order to perfect their craft.

When they're on the court, they make the game look so easy. This is because they've spent hours upon hours mastering their craft while forgoing other activities that they probably wanted to participate in.

Make the necessary sacrifices in your own life. Work tirelessly at your craft or toward your goal so that when your work is presented to the world it looks easy. Make your efforts look effortless. Only when others try to replicate your results will they truly understand how much work you put in and what it took for you to get to where you are.

I know how hard it is to give up the things that you enjoy. It's a constant struggle. I've personally lost too many hours of my own time watching YouTube videos, bingeing TV shows, 'chillin,' scrolling down timelines, or partying with friends. In retrospect, the time I wasted could've been devoted towards doing something productive and beneficial to my future.

Imagine just how much more productive we could be if we made the conscious decision to sacrifice a fraction of the time we devote to leisure or valueless activities and instead chose to do something that will move us closer to our goals. Leisure activities are necessary from time to time. However, too much of anything is not good. Don't waste too much time on unproductive distractions that could be otherwise devoted to securing your future.

The temporary sacrifices you make now will be well worth it when you've arrived in the much better state of being that you've envisioned for yourself. You will never accomplish anything great by only doing things when it is convenient. Convenience kills dreams. Persistence fuels them.

Making sacrifices is difficult; it requires a lot of discipline and prioritization. But you are more than capable of doing so and it will all be worth it in the long run. Once you have accomplished your objectives, you will be able to fully and guiltlessly enjoy all the things you gave up momentarily in addition to reaping the fruits of your labor. So make the necessary sacrifices now in order to realize the life you want. Do today what others won't do so that tomorrow you can have what others can't have.

SECOND QUARTER

4

Use Your Unique Gifts On Your Unique Path

A winner is someone who recognizes his God-given talents, works his tail off to develop them into skills, and uses these skills to accomplish his goal.
LARRY BIRD
3-time NBA champion, 3-time NBA MVP, 12-time NBA All-Star, and a 1998 Naismith Basketball Hall of Fame inductee

We were all born with gifts and talents, whether we have identified them already or not. There are things that you innately do better and more efficiently than anyone else on this earth. This is not just mere speculation, this is a fact. So own that. Embrace it. You have talents that are unique to you and only you.

It is not enough to just be aware of your gifts. You must also cultivate those gifts and use them to your advantage as you embark upon your journey towards accomplishing your goals and living the life that you want to live. Not everyone puts their talents to use or, even more importantly, molds them into skills.

Oftentimes talent gets confused with skill, but the two are not the same. Talent is something that's innate. You are born with the ability to do certain things that come easy to you without much, if any, effort. Contrarily, a skill is a learned behavior that requires you to work hard, persevere, and remain dedicated to refining it. A skill does not require you to be particularly talented at something either. However, if you develop skills that are closely associated with your talents, you are putting yourself in a position to sustain long-term success and master something that is both unique and interesting to you.

As important as it is to use our talents to develop our skill set, a lot of people seem to have an unwillingness to do the required work. We touched on this in the previous chapter. There have been countless top high school basketball prospects that have never played in an NBA game. There are also multitudes of first round draft picks who have ended up being busts in the NBA as well.

Sure there are many reasons why their professional careers didn't pan out, but one of the primary reasons is that they relied solely on their natural abilities and did not work on their games or become skilled at their craft. They may have actually thought that their talent alone would be enough to get them through. Realistically, merely having talent is not enough if you want to be successful in the long run.

One of my favorite parables in the Bible is the parable of the talents in Matthew 24:14-30. Jesus tells of a master who is leaving to go on a trip and entrusts a different amount of talents (currency) to three of his servants. One receives five, another receives two, and the other receives one.

Upon returning to his house, the master finds that the servant with five talents and the one with two talents both flipped what they had and doubled their number of talents. He declared to them, "Well done good and faithful servant. You were faithful over a few things, I will make you ruler over many things."

Conversely, instead of attempting to double the talent he was given, the servant with one talent buried his talent in the ground out of fear of losing it. The master scolded him, called him "wicked and lazy," took the one talent he had away from him, and gave it to the servant who now had 10 talents.

The moral of this parable is that we are rewarded when we use the God-given abilities we have been blessed with in order to advance our lives. If you do more with what you have been given, you will be able to accumulate more. Conversely, if you do nothing with what you have been given, that which you have will be taken away. You can either use what you have or lose what you have. Are you going to put your talents to use or are you just going to waste them away? The choice is yours.

I've personally witnessed people squander their gifts because they were unwilling to do what was necessary in order to cultivate their natural talents into skills. I'm sure you can also name a few individuals who you have seen waste their gifts as well, can't you? There are endless stories of what certain people could have been and what they should have been had they utilized the gifts they were blessed with.

My advice to you is this: do not become yet another "woulda," "coulda," "shoulda" tale. Rather, identify what you are gifted at, work to develop a particular set of skills related to your talents, and make the most out of the natural abilities you have been blessed with in order to live your best life. If you are struggling to identify your gifts, ask yourself a few questions that may help you identify your natural strengths.

"What am I especially good at?"

"What do I do best?"

"What comes easy to me?"

"What is an action that other people compliment me about regularly?"

Also, ask your parents, peers, mentors, coaches, teachers, and those close to you what they believe your strengths are and what you are gifted at. Feedback from others can be a critical piece in helping you to identify what you are talented at so that you can find and begin to make your own path.

You may be gifted at cooking, public speaking, or making people laugh. You may be great at working with numbers, sketching people and things, or you can run faster than anyone you know. You may be able to relate to people or you are excellent at writing. Whatever *it* is, you have an extraordinary gift that is waiting to be shared with the world.

Even if you do not recognize it right now, there are things that are unique to you that can help you in your pursuit of living the life you have always wanted to live. Once you identify these gifts, through introspection and consulting those who know you best, then you will be in a position to nurture those gifts and develop them into skills.

After finishing a solid collegiate basketball career at Cal State Fullerton, Bruce Bowen entered the 1993 NBA Draft. Unfortunately, he went undrafted. Between 1993 and 1997, Bowen played professionally overseas and in the CBA for 5 different teams. If you looked up the definition of a 'journeyman' in the dictionary, his name just might be cited as an example.

In 1997, Bowen's fortune began to change when he was signed to a 10-day contract with the Miami Heat. In his NBA debut, he played 1 minute, but the fact remains that he still played. Get this: Out of the 54 players drafted in the 1993 NBA Draft, 11 of them never played a single minute in an NBA game. Bowen had accomplished something that even those who were selected by teams had never done.

Between 1997 and 2001, Bowen had stints with 4 different NBA teams. However, in the 2000-2001 season, he had a breakout year with the Miami Heat in which he logged more minutes and scored more points that season than he did in his first 4 seasons in the league combined. During the 2000-2001 season, he also began to earn the reputation as a lockdown defensive player. As a result of his strong defensive presence, Bowen was named to the NBA's All-Defensive Second Team that season.

In the 2001-2002 NBA season Bowen joined the San Antonio Spurs, a championship caliber team. In San Antonio, he established himself as one of the league's premier perimeter defenders, and was regularly tasked with guarding the opposing teams' best player. From 2001 to 2008, Bowen earned 8 consecutive nominations to the NBA All-Defensive First and Second Team, placed second in voting for the NBA Defensive Player of the Year from 2005 to 2007, and was a part of three San Antonio Spurs NBA championship teams. During those three title seasons, Bowen was in the starting lineup every single game.

In 2012, the San Antonio Spurs retired Bowen's jersey (No. 12), making him the seventh player in the franchise's history to receive that honor. This all happened for a player who, according to his coach in San Antonio, Gregg Popovich, "couldn't dribble and couldn't pass" but he "shot 3s in the corner" and he "played great D [defense]." [iii]

To be in a league full of dynamic, multidimensional athletes, Bruce Bowen's career excelled because he found one specific area to specialize in: strong perimeter defense. As a result, his career panned out better than and lasted longer than a good amount of the 54 players who were selected instead of him in the 1993 NBA Draft. Bowen carved out his own lane and worked to become undeniably skilled in a specific area—defense. He proved that all he needed to do in order to have a storied career in his profession was to acquire a specific skillset. This is what ultimately set him apart from everyone else and allowed him to be successful.

Identify those areas in which you are talented in and find a unique lane that will allow you to experience long-term success. Let Bruce Bowen serve as an example. If he can be successful in a profession with extremely high turnover and he only had one legitimate skill, you can definitely experience success in your own personal and professional endeavors. But first, it is important to develop a set of skills that will set you up for success.

Find your own lane. Hone your skills in a particular arena—preferably one that will allow you to fully utilize the natural talents that you have been blessed with and can be used to your advantage. Why not become a leader or an expert in an arena that you are naturally skilled in and one that interests you? Work hard of course, but also work smart and have fun while doing it. Continually improve yourself in relation to the endeavors that you are pursuing. The more you do so, the greater you improve the likelihood of long-term success.

What's for you is what's for you. It is not for anyone else. Your path is unique to you and only you. As are the tools that you have been blessed with in order to actualize the life that you have envisioned for yourself. Others have paved their own way and you have the ability to do so yourself in a particular area.

You have something special and unique to bring to the world that no one else does. Take this book, for example. There are thousands of self-help books that have been published throughout history to help us in our journey to achieve our goals. However, I truly believe that no one else could have written this particular book in this particular way except for me. By no means am I bragging or boasting. What I am trying to communicate to you is that the task of writing this book was designated to me exclusively. There can be someone out there with the exact same title, the exact same principles and even the exact same examples, but it will never be the same book. The task of writing this book was given to me specifically by God to bring into existence and share with the world.

The same goes for you—God has called you to produce or to do something that only you can do. Regardless of the magnitude of the contribution. No matter how seemingly small or large, during your time on this earth you are destined to accomplish something that only you are meant to do.

It is extremely important for you to operate daily in a space where you truly believe that you have something that sets you apart and that you were created to leave a positive and unique footprint on this world. Declare this truth to yourself. Remind yourself often that you have something unique to contribute to the world.

Failure to recognize your ability to positively impact your own life and society as a whole can prompt you to begin looking outward. And when you look outward instead of inward, you fall prey to distractions that take you away from your own individual path, resulting in discouragement about your own prospects.

In the age that we live in, particularly because of the wide usage and notoriety of social media, we often see others flaunt their material belongings, routinely recount their own success stories, or even just outright brag about what they have and what they have accomplished. This can cause those of us who are still trying to figure things out and find our way to become disheartened if our life does not "measure up" to the lives that others are projecting on television and on social media.

Between the ages of 22 and 25, I could not find a job in my field of study. Well, the word "find" is kind of generous. It was more like no employer in my field would hire me. I had already earned my bachelor's degree and would go on to earn my master's degree during that time period but still, every single job I applied that had any relation to my major turned me down.

As a result, in order to make ends meet, I had to take whatever employment I could find. And the only place that would hire me was CVS Pharmacy. With two college degrees in hand I was working at CVS stocking shelves, unloading trucks, and taking out trash. Every single day.

I recall becoming discouraged at times because I was broke, living paycheck to paycheck, dwelling in small basement apartments, borrowing from friends and loved ones, trying to find my way, and wondering why the majority of my peers were seemingly thriving while I was struggling. But I had to remind myself, and sometimes still have to, that I am on my own unique path. Which means I am on a unique timetable and that what others are doing has absolutely no impact on what is destined for me.

Had it not been for that period of my life, I would not be the person I am today. I wouldn't have a secure job in my field of study. I wouldn't have started my own nonprofit organization working with youth in low-income communities. I wouldn't be traveling the world at my leisure. Lastly, I certainly wouldn't be in a position to write this book. My unique path has prepared me for where I am today.

What's for you is what's for you, when it's for you. Where you are currently in life is prepping you for who you are destined to become. When discouragement looms and you begin comparing your life to the lives of others, always remember that their life is their life. Their lane is their lane. Their definition of success is different than your definition of success.

While it's great that others are flourishing and succeeding, they have their own path that is completely separate from yours. What good does comparing your life to someone else's do when you are each doing and want completely different things, and are on completely different paths? *None.* Unless those people can help you get to where you want to be, there is no reason to concern yourself with what they are doing.

To take it a step further, who is to say that those whose lives you covet are even doing all the things they say they are doing or actually have the things they say they have? It's unfortunate that this point has to be made, but this is the era in which we live. People often fabricate their lives for the sake of being noticed and garnering attention.

A lot of people talk about what they are going to do all the time, but you never see results. Don't be that person. As Matthew 7:16 (NIV) says, "By their fruit you will recognize them." We don't get recognized for all the things we talk about we are going to do. We are recognized by the actions we carry out and the processes we see all the way through. Think about it, if you personally know people who put on facades, what makes you think that people who you only know because of social media, or YouTube channels, or television shows aren't doing the exact same thing?

My intent is not to belittle anyone. Like the Queen of Hip-Hop Soul Mary J. Blige said, there's no "hateration" or any "holleration in this danceree." I'm all for the glow up. However, you could possibly be comparing yourself to people who are only putting up a front to make their life seem better than it really is. Unconsciously, you may be coveting a quality of life that is less than the one you're currently living.

Comparing yourself and your capabilities to others not only steals the joy that you have within yourself but it also distracts you from the unique path that is in front of you.

While you are still in the process of figuring your life out or working on the goals you have set for yourself, it may be necessary to delete your social media apps, stop watching channels and shows, or cease talking to certain people so that you don't lose focus on your own unique path. Also, so you aren't tempted to compare your walk to others. Protect your path and your vision by any means necessary.

In whatever you do, don't let what other people are doing, whether truthfully or dishonestly, distract you from your own unique path and purpose.

Now, when you find your own lane and set out on your path, do believe there are going to be a lot of naysayers. Everyone who you encounter is not going to like you. Many are not going to be on board with the endeavors you pursue or the moves that you make. Most are not going to celebrate you. They're not going to dap you up. They are not going to shout you out. Shoot, they probably won't even acknowledge that they see what you are doing and instead will critique you and talk about you behind your back. But you know what? Who. Really. Cares? Someone else's opinion or approval of you is quite frankly none of your business.

Take Russell Westbrook, for example. Westbrook is one of the most unique and unapologetic players in the NBA today. From the interesting fashion decisions he makes to how he interacts so candidly and honestly with reporters and the expressive and explosive way he competes every single game, Russell Westbrook is clearly in a world of his own.

In March of 2017, soda brand Mountain Dew premiered a commercial featuring Westbrook. In the commercial, Westbrook runs through a laundry list of things that people tell him not to do. The commercial concludes with him about to perform a motorcycle stunt involving a ramp and a flaming basketball hoop, however, right before he takes off on the motorcycle, he takes a sip of Mountain Dew (of course) and declares, "Don't do they, do you."

This "do you" approach that Westbrook abides by has obviously worked out for him on the court. In the 2016-2017 NBA season, Westbrook became only the second player in NBA history to average a triple double (at least 10 points, 10 rebounds and 10 assists) for an entire season, he broke the long standing record for the most triple doubles in a season, and he won the regular season Most Valuable Player award, all while leading his team to the playoffs. Not only that, but he appears to be living his best life off the court as well, with little regard for anything critics or spectators have to say about him.

People are going to talk, but the beauty of life is that you have no obligation to listen to anything they say. Embrace the fact that what you do with your life isn't about anyone else. It is about being who you are destined to be, making the most of the time you have been blessed with on this earth, and doing what God placed in your heart to do. Too often, people miss their calling, bypass opportunities, or don't do the things they really want to do simply because of how they think they will be perceived or what others will say. They fear looking silly or getting the "I told you so" from spectators if things don't necessarily go the way they initially envisioned.

There's a way to avoid this: Until you accomplish your goal, hold off from talking about it. Make moves, not announcements. When you make announcements, you attract unnecessary attention that may have an adverse effect on your path. Just go after what you want and let your results do the talking for you.

Your dream is yours and only yours—no one else's. Be selective of who you talk to about your goals or plans. Sometimes it is best to keep things to yourself until you accomplish what it is you set out to accomplish because you never know the extent of anyone else's malicious intent.

Feedback and good counsel are extremely important and beneficial. None of us have all the answers. But you have to discern whether that criticism is constructive or fruitless. You also have to evaluate the source from which that criticism/advice is coming from. Examine their fruit *then* decide whether or not you need to take what they are saying with a grain of salt. It will not benefit you to listen to someone who hasn't done much with his or her life or who cannot help you get to where you want to be.

You were put on this earth for a reason. You were blessed with certain abilities and you have interests that are specific to you. You have something to offer the world that has never seen before. So when you attempt to fit into the box that society has tried to cram you into, you are doing God, yourself, your family, and society a disservice. Don't deprive yourself of your highest and fullest life experience. God created you how you are for a reason.

Be comfortable in your own skin. Be unapologetic about who you are. No matter how you may come across to others, stay true to yourself. Don't shrink yourself to fit in. Stand out and shine bright. Block out the unnecessary noise and remain focused on attaining the life that you have envisioned for yourself. Remember, most people are not going to understand you because your gifts and your path are unique to you. Mold your natural abilities into skills, unapologetically go after what you want, and become indifferent to negativity voiced by others regarding your affairs.

This is your life. Live it the way you want to live it. Pursue what it is you want to pursue. And create your own path. Despite the irrelevant opinions of others.

5

See Your Shot Going In Before You Shoot It

Every time I rise up, I have confidence that I am going to make it.
STEPHEN CURRY
3-time NBA champion, 2-time NBA MVP, and 5-time NBA All-Star

As much as preparation, hard work, and sacrifice are important to realizing your dreams and accomplishing your goals, there is another deliberate action we must take that is just as significant as the others: forming a clear mental picture of success prior to attaining it. As you think, so shall you be. It is imperative that you visualize yourself in the state that you want to be in, prior to arriving in that state.

When you have a clear mental picture of what you want and an unbounded desire to accomplish your goal, coupled with putting in the necessary effort, you are actively being drawn towards realizing that goal.

For those of you who played basketball growing up (or any sport for that matter), I'm sure you can recall being encouraged and instructed by your coaches, trainers, and parents to be confident in your ability to score and to perform effectively. Confidence is engrained in athletes from little league all the way up to the highest level of competitive play. Having confidence in your abilities and seeing yourself scoring prior to doing so is key to improving the likelihood of scoring, and ultimately winning.

As you are encouraged to believe in yourself on the court and on the playing field, believe that you are able to do whatever you put your mind to in everything you do.

To further emphasize the importance of having confidence and visualizing success prior to attaining it, several studies have been conducted utilizing basketball in order to test the power of visualization.

One of the most notable sport-based studies on visualization was conducted in 1996 by Dr. Judd Biasiotto of the University of Chicago. Biasiotto split a random grouping of students into three different groups and had them shoot free throws. After they shot their free throws, he then gave each group a specific assignment.

The first group had to practice shooting free throws every day. The second group could not touch a ball and was instructed to do nothing. The third group could not touch a basketball just like the second group but had to visualize themselves shooting and making each one of their free throws every day. After 30 days, the three groups reconvened and Dr. Biasiotto had them shoot the same number of free throws as before.

The first group that practiced shooting every day improved their free throw percentage by 24 percent.

The second group that was prohibited from practicing showed no improvement in their free throw percentage.

The third group that did not practice but was instructed to simply visualize making free throws in their mind improved their free throw shooting percentage by 23 percent.

The results from the study suggest that visualizing yourself making free throws is just as effective as practicing free throws.[iv] This infers that seeing yourself accomplishing something prior to undertaking it has a positive impact on the likelihood of being successful at that endeavor.

Knowing this, imagine how much more likely you are to accomplish your goals if you visualize yourself in the state you want to be in *and* you put in the necessary work to get there. You would be pretty much unstoppable!

See and feel yourself in the specific state that you want to be in. Channel the emotions that are attached to being in your desired state—feelings of happiness, accomplishment, and fulfillment. Walk like it. Talk like it. Dress like you are already working in your dream vocation. Talk to friends about places you have booked to travel to in the future. Buy clothes (or put them in your online cart) that are at your desired size at the end of your fitness journey. Act as if you are already where you want to be in life.

One of the most underutilized yet effective moves that a basketball player can perform is the pump fake. The pump fake allows players to get their opponents off of their feet, clearing the way for an easy basket for themselves or for their teammate. The pump fake also increases a player's chances of drawing a foul on their opponent while in the act of shooting, thus putting them on the free throw line to shoot one-to-three uncontested free throws. You are merely acting as if you are going to try to score, but when you pump fake, it is all a ploy to deceive the defender to improve your likelihood of scoring.

Start doing your own pump faking. Deceive your subconscious defenders (fear, ego, doubt, etc.) so that you push negative thoughts and emotions to the side that have the potential to block you from progressing towards living your best life.

Imagine how it would feel if you were in the state you wanted to be in or had the things that you desire and attach yourself to the emotions that correspond to that state or possession. Hold on to that feeling throughout your day. Whatever it is that puts you in the space to receive the results you desire, do those things. (Pump) fake it, until you make it.

Adopt this approach in all applicable areas of your life that you want to see change in. Your thoughts and your emotions are the greatest barometers to how you are fairing in life and ultimately affect your outlook on the future. Getting control of your thoughts and emotions now and only accepting positivity are steps toward living the life that you aspire to live. Hold on to those positive thoughts and emotions while putting in the necessary work to attain what you want.

Live expectantly. Have the expectation that great things are supposed to happen to you. Believe that good things are supposed to happen and anticipate that what you want will come to pass in your life regardless of the circumstances or situations that you are currently in.

You may think this sounds silly and I'm sure some of you right now are probably questioning the legitimacy of this approach. Well, as we've done thus far, let's relate this principle back to basketball.

Say you are playing ball and you happen to be in a shooting slump. What are some of the thoughts that are going through your head?

No matter what I do, I can't buy a bucket.

It's just not my game.

I'm having an off day.

How do you feel when you're in a shooting slump? More than likely you feel disappointed, defeated, discouraged, and helpless, correct? When you choose to embrace these negative thoughts and emotions while you're experiencing your shooting slump doesn't it seem like things get progressively worse and worse?

On the contrary, what if you're on a hot shooting streak? It's the complete opposite. You're in the zone. You believe that anything you put in the air is going to go through the hoop. The ball is basically a pebble and the basket is the ocean. You even have "heat checks"—shooting shots you wouldn't usually take but you are more confident now because everything is going your way. You feel accomplished, ecstatic, and unstoppable. You feel like anything can and will go your way.

In life—on or off the court—whether you choose to embrace positive thoughts and emotions or you choose to embrace negative thoughts and emotions, based on your decision, one or the other is going to manifest in your life experiences. Why not choose a positive mindset and good vibes only while pursuing your dreams?

Yes, it is easier said than done but if you make a habit of thinking and feeling positively, regardless of your circumstances, you will be able to bounce back and continue on your path.

Change your thoughts and your mood and see how your outcomes begin to change as well. Choose a life that is consistent with the thoughts and emotions you would have when you're in a shooting zone, not one that mirrors the thoughts and emotions you would have during a shooting slump. Live in a constant state of expectation and truly believe that what you want will happen in your life. Always expect your shot to go in.

Visualize yourself accomplishing your goals and feel yourself in that state of accomplishment before and during your journey. Go throughout your day with the utmost confidence that the positive mental picture of your life that you have constructed will materialize in the real world.

That which we focus our thoughts and our feelings upon is what we will attract into our lives. This concept is most commonly referred to as the law of attraction and is true for both positive and negative thoughts. Everything that we see in the world around us is the visible expression of the thoughts that we have had.

That means the place that we live in, the people who we associate with, the job that we have, and so on and so forth are all extensions of the thoughts we've had at some point in our lives. What we give our energy to is what we attract and what manifests itself into our life experience.

Sometimes negative thoughts are going to creep into our minds. It is part of the human experience. However, once this occurs, immediately filter out those toxic thoughts and shift your focus back onto only what you want.

Even if things are not necessarily going your way, when you focus on thoughts of increase, productivity, success, and happiness, you will attract all of those things into your life. On the other hand, if you focus on loss, wasted time, failure, or sadness, those things will inevitably appear.

Your thoughts hold the power of life or loss. Make it a habit to focus your energy on what it is that you want instead of what you do not want. Screening your thoughts and monitoring your feelings are critical preliminary steps toward changing your life and, as a result experiencing the outcomes that you want and deserve. By no means will this be an easy feat. In fact, it will be a struggle at first. You will have to block out all the negativity that routinely bombards your life and break from the toxic thought conditioning that you have adhered to for so long.

At some point, by consistently doing an inventory of your thoughts and making the conscious effort to focus on the things that only bring you joy, peace, and happiness, your life will begin to change for the better. Just like ballplayers expect the ball to go into the hoop when they shoot it, expect for the things that you want in your life to come to fruition as well.

A spiritual extension of confidence, expectation, acting as-if, and positive thinking is faith—the unwavering belief that a Higher Power is guiding us and moving us in the direction of living our best lives. According to Hebrews 11:1 (NIV), faith is *"confidence* in what we hope for and *assurance* about what we do not see." Faith guides us on our way to becoming our best selves, accomplishing our goals, and realizing our purpose—even when things may not seem to be going in our favor.

Right now, you may not be able to confidently fathom walking across the stage and receiving that diploma in your hands, or viewing your optimal goal weight on the scale, or being able to withdraw a specific dollar amount from your bank account when you'd like, or picking up your bestselling book from a bookshelf in the store. However, if you maintain an unwavering faith, believing that a Higher Power is interceding on your behalf in all ways, then those things will soon come to pass.

Our lives are guided by divine influence. This means that no matter your circumstances or present state, at the end of it all, you are going to be alright. What you want in your life *will* come to pass. Just as long as you have faith that it will. As Matthew 17:20 (NIV) states, "If you have faith as small as a mustard seed, you can say to this mountain, 'Move from here to there,' and it will move. Nothing will be impossible for you." Nothing at all.

6
Shoot Your Shot...And Always Follow Through

You can't get much done in life if you only work on the days when you feel good.
JERRY WEST
14-time NBA All-Star, 1972 NBA champion, a 1980 Naismith Basketball Hall of Fame inductee, and 'The Logo' of the NBA

How many of you have been a spectator at a youth league basketball game? I'm talking about the games that 6- and 7-year-olds play in. Correct me if I'm wrong, but those games have the potential to be the most hectic 24 minutes you could ever watch. Not one set play is run. Kids in oversized jerseys and shorts are just running around, pummeling into each other. Some of them may even pick up the ball and start running with it or mistakenly attempt to score on the wrong basket.

And if one of them sees just a tiny sliver of daylight towards the basket, you better believe they're going to catapult the ball from their hip, their stomach, or even from behind their heads towards the hoop.

All of that action (more like distress for us spectators) and the final score ends up being something like 17 to 12 or 9 to 4. Bless their hearts.

The little ones have it right in one regard though: You have to start somewhere.

Every great player has started at that same point of just chucking the ball up towards the rim with the hope that it will go in. And although the majority of the shots that the kids take either ricochet off the backboard, clang off the rim, or hit nothing at all, they consistently live by the code to relentlessly *shoot your shot*. Maybe, just maybe, the occasional shot will go in and they will score.

There's an old saying that goes, *if you hang around the barbershop long enough, eventually you'll get a haircut.* In this case, *if you shoot your shot enough times, eventually your shot will go in.*

Sometimes you're not going to have a clue as to how to approach a task or get started on a specific endeavor. But the mere fact that you're willing to try brings you that much closer to accomplishing that task.

You miss all of the shots you don't take. It is better to at least try to accomplish something than to not do anything at all. Whether you choose to go after what you want and fail *or* you choose to not go after it at all, you will still yield the same results. Why not at least take a chance and go after what you want to increase the likelihood of being in a better place than where you currently are? You really have nothing to lose yet only something to gain.

The worst thing that can happen when you go after what you want is that you fail. Big deal. Your life isn't over. Even when you fail, you have an endless amount of attempts left to succeed. Eventually, if you continue to shoot your shot, your shot is going to go in. The game is rigged in your favor. It's not over until you win!

So when you're pursuing your goals, keep shooting. Keep striving. Keep working. Keep persevering. That is the only way you will be able to accomplish your objectives. If you do fail (which you will at some point) at least you will be able to say you gave it everything you had, you went out shooting, and you have no regrets. There is nothing worse than looking back on your life regretting not doing something that was placed in your heart to do.

The fear of failure is what often holds people back from doing the things they want to do and prevents them from experiencing the happiness they desire. Fear is the misuse of our creative capacity. We spend so much time fearing things we cannot control and things that will probably never happen. As a result, we hold ourselves back from creating the life we want.

When we do actually go after what we want and fail initially, we often want to give up. We feel like it's not worth the pain or the hassle and that trying to accomplish a particular objective may be a waste of our time. Or sometimes we let intimidation get the best of us. We begin doubting our capabilities. We start convincing ourselves the feat we are trying to accomplish is greater than our ability to do so. As a result, we become discouraged and stop going after what we truly want.

Instead of being fearful, intimidated, or discouraged, be excited and optimistic about the opportunity to utilize your creativity to accomplish the things you desire. The life that you want for yourself is one that is more than feasible.

Anything you truly want and anything you are putting considerable effort into attaining is not a waste of time. You may only think you are wasting your time because things are not going the way you initially anticipated they would. Guess what? Life isn't easy. It's hard. The most convenient option is to give up and avoid the pain. But the rewarding alternative is to push past your missed attempts and through the pain to get to where you want to be. As Galatians 6:9b (NIV) says, "for at the right time we will reap a harvest if we do not give up." Keep shooting your shot until your shot goes in.

There is no point in playing it safe in this life. We are all going to die eventually. Sorry for being so blunt but it's the truth. Being cognizant of this absolute fact of life, how are you going to proceed?

You have two choices. You can sit up in the stands, filled with regret and slowly wither away, and watch as others shoot their shot, make things happen, and have fun *or* you can get on the court, shoot your shots, make things happen, and have fun for yourself. It is completely up to you. Only you can make the decision regarding the type of person you want to be—either a spectator or a player. My hope is that for the remainder of your time here on this earth, you choose to get in the game and strive for the life you've envisioned for yourself.

There have been days for everyone when you don't feel like doing something critical to the advancement towards your goal. Tomorrow, the weekend, or sometime next week always seem to be the better option, don't they? However, none of those days are promised to us. All we have is the present to get done what needs to get done.

In basketball, what is key to an effective jump shot is that when you do shoot your shot, you maintain your follow through. Your follow through on your jump shot is vital for a variety of reasons.

The follow through is basically a measuring stick for your shot. When you shoot your shot and you follow through, you get to gauge how much strength and effort is needed to shoot the ball at different distances from the basket. The better understanding you have of your shot, the greater likelihood you have of scoring.

Just like the follow through when you shoot a basketball, your follow through on tasks pertaining to your endeavors is guiding you towards your desired outcome. Your degree of effort and persistence while attempting to complete your goal allows you to gauge what is needed to complete your objective.

At certain points in time, you will have to work a little harder, a little faster, or a little smarter in order to accomplish your goal. You may get tired. You may get discouraged. You may even want to give up. By remaining committed to the process, you will be able to see what it is going to take in order to get you closer to your goal.

The follow through on your jump shot is also important because the backspin on the ball caused by the snap of your wrist at the end of the follow through can help the ball get that friendly bounce around the rim and into the hoop. This bounce has come to be characterized as the 'shooter's roll.'

As you consistently put in the time and the effort to accomplish your goals, you may have a breakthrough that will help you meet your mark faster than you would have initially thought. Call it luck, call it favor (which I do), call it whatever you want. When you are consistently performing actions with the intent to make your life better and you continue to stick it out despite your circumstances or the occurrence of setbacks, you get breaks that help push you further in the right direction. All because you remained dedicated to the process and followed through on your initial efforts.

Whether it's someone offering their help to you, or funds become available at the bank for that desired business loan, or a specific product that you would otherwise not be able to afford goes on sale, or you make valuable connections at an event you were invited to by a friend or colleague. Whatever the case may be, this "friendly bounce" in life is only possible when you remain steadfast, when you keep your commitment to your commitment, and when you follow through with the efforts that are necessary to accomplishing your goals.

Your follow through is also a means of aiming your shot at the basket. You are essentially guiding your shot into the hoop. I talked earlier about kids and how they just throw the ball up at the hoop any way they are able to. Yeah I know, they don't have the strength yet to properly shoot the ball but because of this, they are not following through with their shot and, in turn, are not aiming at the basket. Thus, most times their shot ends up going any and everywhere, except in the hoop, each time they shoot. Your objective is to put the ball into the basket so making sure your shooting hand falls toward the rim each time you shoot is a means of aiming your shot at the rim.

If you do not have a clear aim or a detailed plan for how you are going to accomplish your goals, then you will soon lose sight of what it is you are trying to accomplish. It will just become another brilliant idea that was thought up, put on the shelf, and forgotten about. Specifically define what it is that you want so that you will be able to discern exactly what is necessary in order to attain it. By mapping out what you need to do, you are guiding yourself towards your end goal as you have established a timeline and a game plan for your particular endeavor.

Lastly, the follow through on a jump shot helps you to keep the same shooting form every time you shoot. Consistency is key. Without maintaining a consistent shooting form, your shot will change every time you shoot the ball, decreasing your chances of making your shot. When you adhere to proper shooting mechanics consistently, you ingrain those mechanics into your muscle memory. You are creating an effective habit through repetition that will ultimately result in success with your shot. After a while, you won't even have to think about your form or your follow through. It will become ingrained and automatic.

We are what we repeatedly do. Form good habits in your life that become second nature. Repetition develops skill that can be used to assist you on your path towards accomplishing your goals. If you consistently put in the work to accomplish a certain goal, then you will eventually accomplish said goal.

Shooting your shot and following through on your shot isn't about doing everything perfectly. No one is able to do everything perfectly all the time. Sometimes you will have to do things in an unorthodox way and get creative in order for you to attain your goals. Just because your approach is different does not mean it is doomed for failure. It is just your own unique way of doing things.

Step out on faith and remain dedicated to completing what you set your mind to. Tirelessly beat on your craft, remain consistent in the pursuit of your goal, and see the process through to the end regardless of any obstacles or impediments that may present themselves. Follow through with your initial actions until your objective is completed.

The accomplishment of your goal is dependent on the actions you carry out consistently on the path towards attaining that goal. It is not how you start, it is how you finish. It is about repetition. It is about having a clear direction and plan for your life. It is about putting yourself in a position to receive unexpected blessings. It is about evaluating whether the level of effort you are putting in or the actions you are carrying out are getting you closer to your mark.

If you want to attain your desired outcomes in life, it is imperative that you put in the work on a continual and consistent basis—even on the days that you really don't feel like doing anything. The reality is, if you keep putting off certain tasks until a later time, they will more than likely never get done. Then, you will be left wondering why your life hasn't panned out the way you wanted it to. Which points to one thing and one thing only—you didn't keep your commitment to your commitment.

Never put off until tomorrow what you are capable of doing today. Procrastination is a productivity and, ultimately, a dream killer. Always remember, the words "I don't feel like it" never resulted in anything great.

Of course, you should absolutely take the time to rest, recuperate, and get in tune with your star player (You). A vacation (or even a "staycation") is needed every once in a while. It will allow you to be refreshed and renewed, ready to get back to working on your goal.

One of my favorite quotes from my favorite book *The Alchemist* by Paulo Coelho goes, "Rest a little, but as soon as you can, get up and carry on. Because ever since your goal found out that you were traveling toward it, it has been running to meet you."[v] Take as much time as you need to get in tune with yourself and to enjoy life, but never lose sight of your goals and don't put them off for too long.

I'll be honest with you—there are instances when I'm not up to writing (like right now). I'd much rather be relaxing, doing something else, or better yet, doing absolutely nothing. However, my goal is to finish writing this book and the only action that will allow me to get closer to completing that goal is to write, consistently, even when I do not feel like it (like right now).

Life has a tendency to get in the way. We get bombarded with work, we lose inspiration, we're tired, we're frustrated, we have to deal with relationship and family issues, and at times we have pressing affairs to address. I understand this completely. Yet the fact of the matter is, for as long as we exist on this earth, stuff is going to happen. Things will pop up. Unfavorable events will occur. It's inevitable. However, you can't push your commitments to the side just because something is not necessarily going your way or you feel like being lazy. Consistency is key if you want to realize the life that you've always envisioned for yourself.

Remain committed to your dreams. Follow through on your initial efforts towards your desired outcome. See your goal through until it is accomplished regardless of what may be thrown in your path along the way. That is the only way you can attain the life that you want. For you are blessed and rewarded when you stay on the course, not when you stop and give up.

Whatever it is that you want to do and accomplish, remain true and committed to the process. Shoot your shot, and always follow through.

HALFTIME

First Half Highlights

We are halfway through the book! Thank you for making it this far! Before we continue, I wanted to take a quick break (like halftime in an actual game) and briefly highlight a few key takeaways from the 1st half. We will have a section similar to this after the 2nd half of the book as well.

Remove Limitations

- Your age, race, gender, demographic background, or socioeconomic status have nothing to do with what you are able to accomplish—only you do.
- Do not rule yourself out of attaining greatness without even attempting to tap into the unbounded potential that exists within you.
- Nothing outside of yourself has the power to dictate your outcomes in life. Do not downgrade your dreams to fit someone else's reality.

Take Responsibility For Your Own Outcomes

- Only when you accept responsibility for your outcomes will you be able to change them.

- You are where you are in life solely because of the decisions you made and the actions you carried out.
- Making excuses and assigning blame are means of avoiding responsibility. Take ownership of your own stuff.

Put In The Work And Prepare Adequately

- In order to be successful at anything in life, you must prepare adequately.
- How you do the small things will be how you do the big things. No task is too minor. The degree to which you prepare is always seen in your results.
- It is better to be prepared for an opportunity and not have one than to have an opportunity and not be prepared.

Use Your Unique Gifts On Your Unique Path

- You have talents that are unique to you. It is not enough to simply be aware of your talents, but you must cultivate them into skills.
- Comparison is the thief of joy. Don't compare your life or your path to those of others. Protect your path and vision by any means necessary.

- Your life and what you do is not about anyone else. It is about making the most of your time on earth and doing what God called you to do.

See Your Shot Going In Before You Shoot It

- Have confidence in yourself that you are able to attain whatever you put your mind to. Form a clear mental picture of success prior to attaining it. As you think, so shall you be.
- Act as if you are already where you want to be in life. Pump fake it until you make it.
- Have faith that a Higher Power is guiding you and moving you in the direction of living your best life.

Shoot Your Shot...And Always Follow Through

- You miss all of the shots you don't take. It is better to at least try than to not do anything at all. Keep shooting your shot until your shot goes in.
- Follow through on all of your initial efforts. By doing so, you will eventually accomplish your feat.
- You are what you repeatedly do. Consistency is key if you want to realize the life you have envisioned for yourself.

THIRD QUARTER

7

Success Leaves Clues

You've got to study all the greats. You've got to learn what made them successful and what made them unsuccessful.
MICHAEL JACKSON
13-time Grammy Award winner, double inductee into the Rock and Roll Hall of Fame, the 'King of Pop,' and mentor to LA Lakers great Kobe Bryant

I mentioned earlier that the only people you should regularly concern yourself with are those who can help you accomplish your goals and objectives. While it is absolutely true that we were all born with unique gifts that are specific to us, it is also true that at some point in history, there has been at least one other person who has successfully accomplished goals that are similar, if not practically identical, to the ones that we have set for ourselves. Now, because of technological advancements, we have access to these individuals in one way or another. What a time, to be alive.

In the pursuit of the successful completion of goals, experiences are shared. Knowing this truth, you should make it a priority to study the habits, the decisions, and the tendencies of those who have succeeded in the areas in which you aspire to succeed.

What exactly is it is that you want to accomplish? What kind of life do you aspire to build for yourself? Once you've determined what your aspirations are and what it is that you want to do with your life, research the people who have effectively done those things. If you do so, you will essentially have a ready-made blueprint from successful individuals on what it takes to successfully complete that particular endeavor.

There is nothing new under the sun. Individuals whose path was similar to yours have existed (or even still do) and they had to carry out specific steps in order to succeed. Why not use their successful model as a guide in your own personal pursuit of that similar goal?

If we look at the NBA, the most obvious example of a player taking facets of another player's game is Kobe Bryant.

Since he first entered the NBA in 1996, Bryant has been compared to none other than the greatest to ever play the game—Michael Jordan. The patented fade away, the fist pump, the killer mentality; it was as if Kobe was Michael Jordan 2.0. But that particular MJ wasn't Kobe's most notable teacher. The person who Kobe deemed as the "greatest influence" of his life was actually the King of Pop—Michael Jackson.

The summer after Bryant's rookie season, Michael Jackson reached out to the younger Bryant to tell him that he had been studying him and wanted to offer advice, insight, and materials that Bryant would go on to utilize in order to mold himself into one of the greatest players to ever play the game. Jackson explicitly told Bryant the words used in the quote at the beginning of this chapter: "You've got to study all the greats. You've got to learn what made them successful and what made them unsuccessful." That's exactly what the self-proclaimed "thief" did.

Kobe became the ultimate student of the game. He adapted Jerry West's quick release, studied Elgin Baylor's footwork, and stole Oscar Robertson's pump fake. After a 33-point outing against Michael Jordan and the Chicago Bulls in December 1997, Jordan approached Kobe after the game and told him that if he ever needed anything, to give him a call. The rest was history. According to Bryant, "speaking to MJ was like getting my own college education at the highest level."

Further heeding the advice of Jackson, Bryant would go on to reach out to and build relationships with other NBA greats including Bill Russell, Magic Johnson, Larry Bird, Hakeem Olajuwon, and Kareem Abdul-Jabbar—soaking up all the information and insight he could from these legends.[vi]

Consequently, Bryant had one of the most storied careers in NBA history and was consistently effective over the course of his 20-year career. His success can be partially accredited to the fact that he studied and built relationships with select individuals who found success in the NBA prior to him entering the league.

Not only can you learn from your predecessors, but you can also learn from your peers and some unlikely sources.

If I was to do a survey and asked who had the deadliest crossover dribble in the NBA between 1996 and 2011, which player do you think most people would say? They would probably (hopefully) go with Hall of Famer and Philadelphia 76ers legend Allen Iverson. Iverson made defenders, including

Michael Jordan and Kobe Bryant, look silly with his patented crossover. But you'll never guess from whom Iverson learned his crossover (unless you're an avid A.I. fan and already know).

Allen Iverson learned his crossover, not from a collegiate All-American or an NBA All-Star; he learned it from his college teammate at Georgetown University, walk-on Dean Berry. Berry was a member of the team yes, but he was also the last player on the team's depth chart. Iverson often recounts that he used to have to guard Berry in practice and Berry would get him with the same crossover move every single time, even when he knew it was coming.

Iverson realized how effective the move was and knew that if he incorporated the crossover into his repertoire, it could take his game to a higher level than it already was. So, Iverson eventually swallowed his pride and asked Berry to teach him the move.[vii] The result? Iverson made countless opponents look silly throughout the duration of his collegiate and Hall of Fame NBA career. All from a move he learned from his walk-on, end-of-the-bench sitting college teammate.

Most basketball fans know that Berry didn't create the crossover, however, he mastered his own version by taking different components of the crossover from other players, most notably NBA legend Tim Hardaway.

Tim Hardaway created his own form of the crossover dribble by taking components of former Syracuse University standout Pearl Washington's crossover.[viii] I'm sure Washington mastered his own crossover from observing the moves of other players and created his own version from there.

Success leaves clues. There is always something you can learn from someone else, whether he or she is your predecessor or your peer, which will put you in a better position to be successful in your endeavors.

Don't allow your ego to deter you from learning something from someone that can ultimately change your life. Seek out guidance from someone who can help you and you will end up in a far better place than you were before you sought his or her counsel.

Unfortunately, we live in a society where many people want to tout themselves as "self-made," asserting that they've attained success all on their own, with no help. Too often we do not ask pertinent questions or seek insight and guidance because we think we know it all and our ego rationalizes that if someone else can do it on their own, we can do it on our own too. This rhetoric and way of thinking essentially discourages collaboration, limits the capacity for results, and devalues one of the greatest tools for success—mentorship.

Like NBA players, you have your own unique gifts and your own lane in which you are most effective. But similar to how players have taken other player's moves to incorporate into their game and use to their advantage, you can increase the likelihood of being successful in your own life by taking certain things from others who have achieved similar feats as those which you desire to achieve. Even renowned artist Pablo Picasso said, "good artists borrow, great artists steal." (I bet you twenty dollars that he stole that line from someone else.)

Take what you can from others that will help you to accomplish the goals you have set for yourself. If given the opportunity, spend as much time as possible in the company of those who are where you want to be so you can pick their brains, adopt their techniques, observe their tendencies, and use the knowledge they impart to you to your own benefit. Some of these individuals may be a phone call away. Some may be available for you to shadow at work. Some you may be able to message via email or through a social media platform. Others you may have to just follow their example from afar through YouTube videos, articles, books, or interviews.

I have mentors who I am able to talk to directly via phone, text, and in person, and pick their brains and learn from them. I also have mentors, such as actor Will Smith, media mogul Oprah Winfrey, motivational speaker and author Les Brown, and music executive and entrepreneur Sean "Diddy" Combs, who I am currently unable to get in contact with but I have still gained tremendous insight from them via social media, interviews, books, movies, and podcasts.

Whatever avenue is available to you, seek guidance from those who are where you want to be so that you can accomplish your goals in an efficient manner.

If you want a stable, well-paying career, seek out those who work in the field that you aspire to work in, build a good rapport with them, and learn what it takes to obtain employment in that specific field.

If you want a healthy marriage, build a relationship with couples who have been married for many years, have weathered difficult times, and who can offer advice and guidance on what makes a marriage longstanding and successful.

If you want to lose weight, consult with those who have gone through a weight loss transformation, have consistently maintained their physique, stayed in good health, and can provide you with eating and training regimens that have proven results.

If you want to run a thriving business, find someone who runs a profitable business, study their business plan, and pick their brain regarding what they did to keep their business afloat in an ever-changing economy.

What about the individuals who you aspire to learn from but are unreachable? Read books and articles written by them or about them, subscribe to their blogs, email lists, and channels, follow them on social media, listen to their interviews, or watch their biopics. There are a myriad of mediums available for you to learn from those you aspire to emulate without it being a direct, personal interaction.

Whether they are accessible or inaccessible, there are people who can help you on your path to attaining the life you want. You just have to do the legwork in gaining the beneficial insight from them in whatever manner you are able to.

Where you are right now—mapping out your plan, trying to find an effective way to go about accomplishing your goals, and maneuvering past, through, and over obstacles—someone has been before. Most, if not all, people who have followed their dreams have encountered difficulties on their own personal journeys. They have received many bumps and bruises along the way. Who better to guide you than those who have been through the same challenges you have or may eventually face and have overcome them?

Learning from successful people will provide you with the insight into how to avoid the obstacles that they have previously encountered on their path to success. Or at the very least, lessen the blows that you take. Find out what they have done to catapult themselves to their present state. Try to understand their thought process when approaching different circumstances and situations.

Once you have an understanding of what they did and how they did it, begin incorporating what you've learned from them into your own life to help you along your way. Studying or being in the company of those who you can learn from, and finding out how they attained the things in their lives that you aspire to attain are important components in the formula to living your best life.

Where there is one successful person, you can almost always guarantee that they've had a mentor or a person who has helped them get to where they are. The cycle of learning from those who came before us is continuous. Use it to your advantage. Mentorship is time-tested and proven to be beneficial.

Make a conscious effort to learn from those who can help you get what you want out of life. Don't go through unnecessary struggles just for the sake of being able to say you did it on your own. Especially when you have the resources available to you to help you on your journey. More often than not, people are willing to help you if they see you are serious about bettering your life. Rather than struggling when you really don't have to, seek out guidance from those who are where you want to be so you can attain your goals in a more timely and efficient manner.

There is no need to reinvent the wheel. Just learn from those who have already done it well and improve upon it.

8

Your Dream Is Only As Good As Your Team

Five guys on the court working together can achieve more than five talented individuals who come and go as individuals.
KAREEM ABDUL-JABBAR
6-time NBA champion, 6-time NBA MVP, 19-time NBA All-Star, and a 1995 Naismith Basketball Hall of Fame inductee

Only five players from each team are permitted to be on the court at one time throughout the course of a basketball game. The starting five players for a respective team are usually the five best players on the team at each position (point guard, shooting guard, small forward, power forward, and center). Unless a team has employed a specific strategy tailored to the opponent they are facing, the starting five are usually the players who spend the most time on the court during a game in order to improve the likelihood of victory.

Motivational speaker, author, and entrepreneur Jim Rohn once said, "You are the average of the five people you spend the most time with." Who is in your starting 5? Who are the people you spend the most time hanging with, talking to, and consequently, are being influenced by? Does the presence of these individuals leave you better off? Or does their presence hold you back from realizing your greatest potential?

As important as it is to seek out those who are where you aspire to be and who can help you along your path, it is extremely vital to surround yourself with peers who have the same degree of aspirations for their lives as you do. These are the people you interact with on a regular, if not daily, basis. These are the people you converse with about your life and your goals, issues you may be having, and everything else under the sun. At some point you have to do some inventory of your associations and ask yourself, "Are the people around me adding anything of benefit to my life?"

It is very commonplace to see NBA players with an entourage full of their childhood friends everywhere they go. While some players have great friends who positively contribute to their lives, such as LeBron James and his lifelong friends-turned-business partners, there are an abundance of players who keep people around who are not adding anything to the players' lives in any regard but instead, are taking away from it.

Only sit at the same table with those who have the same appetite as you, not those who are solely at the table because they want what is on your plate. That includes everyone. Friends, family members, and significant others are not exempt.

Surround yourself only with people who force you to become the best version of yourself and want to see you live your best life. Individuals who encourage you to aspire for greatness and become a better person. Those who give you the necessary inspiration to step up, get your stuff in order, and make a meaningful impact. Those who are there when you are putting in the work and do what they are able to do to help you along your path. The ones who are with you shooting in the gym.

By default, who you associate with has a profound impact on the direction your life goes in. In fact, the people you surround yourself with can be the reason why you're not producing any results in your life to begin with. Just because you have a team, that does not guarantee victory—especially if your team is not comprised of the right personnel. If you are constantly surrounded by people who are complacent, destructive, and have no vision for their lives, eventually you will begin to adopt that behavior and lose sight of your own aspirations. Bad company corrupts good character. So take inventory of your associations, evaluate the people in your life, and make adjustments as necessary.

James Harden serves as a good example of minding your associations. Although he averaged 29.0 points per game during the 2015-2016 season (a career high at the time), Harden didn't make any of the All-NBA teams and his team—the Houston Rockets—was eliminated in the first round of the playoffs after barely securing the 8th seed in the Western Conference.

At the end of what he deemed the worst year of his life, Harden and his inner circle gathered together in order to reevaluate his life and his career and came to the determination that adjustments were necessary.

Among other things, he ended his high-profile romantic relationship that brought unnecessary attention and served as a distraction. His high school friends moved out of his house. He chose to train with his collegiate trainer at Arizona State University that summer instead of staying at home in

Los Angeles. He worked with Houston executives to recruit free agents to join the Rockets. He built a better camaraderie with his teammates off the court in order to improve their chemistry and rapport on the court—the lack thereof is what contributed to the team's demise the prior year.[ix]

What were the results? For the 2016-2017 season, Harden averaged 29.1 points, 11.2 assists and 8.1 rebounds per game—all career highs. He earned First-Team All-NBA honors. He was one of three finalists for the league's Most Valuable Player. The Rockets finished with the 3rd best record in the NBA and advanced to the 2nd round of the playoffs before being eliminated. During the 2017-2018 season, Harden led the NBA in scoring at 30.4 points per game, earned First-Team All-NBA honors again, was named league MVP, and led the Rockets to the best record in the NBA, a No.1 seed in the playoffs, and eventually to the Western Conference Finals. When Harden made the decision to make certain changes in his life in regards to the people around him and his interactions with them, not only did his performance improve but the performance of his team did as well.

Teamwork makes the dream work. But your team also has the potential to destroy your dream if those around you aren't elevating you and do not contribute anything of value. Proverbs 27:17 (NIV) says, "As iron sharpens iron, so one person sharpens another." You are only as good as the people whom you consistently surround yourself with.

Let's use a pick-up basketball game to further illustrate this point. Say you're the captain in a random pick-up game at the park or in the gym. You have the desire to win as many games as possible so what are you going to do? Pick the best available players on the court to be on your team, right? You may have even brought a few of your friends with you who can hoop to improve the odds of winning. You are intent on having the best squad so that you can increase your likelihood of winning game after game and remain on the court as long as possible.

What is mindboggling to me is that some of us have a greater desire to win in a pick-up basketball game than we do in winning at life. We will fight to get the best players on our team during a recreational game that doesn't mean much of anything in the grand scheme of things yet, when it really matters, we are content with associating with people who add no value to our lives. The game of life is much more important than a game of basketball. How can you expect to live your best life and win when you team lacks the appropriate personnel to do so? You can't. Your dream is only as good as your team.

The 1992 USA Men's Basketball Team, better known as the "Dream Team," is often referred to as the greatest sports team ever assembled. Comprised of the greatest players in the NBA at the time—and Duke University standout Christian Laettner—the Dream Team competed in the 1992 Olympic games in Barcelona, Spain.

The Dream Team demolished their international competition by an average of 44 points on their way to winning the gold medal. They went 8-0 in Olympic competition. They scored 100 or more points in every single game. The team's head coach, Chuck Daly, did not even call a single timeout in any of the games.

As of today, 11 of the 12 players on the roster have been inducted into the Naismith Basketball Hall of Fame. The 1992 team, as a whole, was enshrined in the Olympic Hall of Fame in 2009 and the Basketball Hall of Fame in 2010.

Each player on the Dream Team possessed his own unique skill set and was the best at what he did on the basketball court. When they were assembled together onto one team, they were unstoppable. Naturally they pushed each other and as a result, brought out the best in one another. That is the by-product of coexisting with greatness.

We are a reflection of the people we surround ourselves with. The more time you spend with people, the more they will begin to rub off on you. And the more they rub off on you, the more you pick up their habits and become like them—regardless of whether they are good influences or bad influences. Those who add no value to your life and are only negative influences can only impede your progress, slow you down, and cause you to remain stagnant. If you truly want to be successful, achieve your goals, and attain happiness, there is absolutely no room in your life for people who do not have your best interests at heart and those who do not provide any value added through your interactions with them.

Be selective with your interactions and whom you choose to spend your time with. You can tell a lot about the future of a person based on the company he or she keeps. So keep those around you who want more out of life with the same passion, the same enthusiasm, and the same intensity as you. Not those who do nothing to build you up, are cynical about your potential for success, or make you question if it is possible to accomplish the goals you set for yourself.

Your goals and interests are not always going to align with those of your friends. But what should be shared is you and your team's level of drive and ambition. You all should have the desire to hold each other accountable and advocate on one another's behalf. Influence and advocacy are not one-sided—they go both ways. If you and your friends are aspiring to be the best you can possibly be, in the respective lanes that you all are in, the example you set for each other should motivate you all to go after your dreams even more. Be a part of a team with unique dreams but an identical grind.

If no one in your circle of friends can help you grow, then it's time for you to find a new group of friends. As the saying goes, "if you're the smartest person in the room, you need to find a new room." You should have the desire to align yourself with people you can learn from and who push you beyond your current circumstances. What exactly can you learn from being around those who have nothing to teach you? I'll tell you what—not anything of value.

What you will learn, however, is how to become a fragment of the person that you are destined to be. You will operate in a space that is lower than your unbounded potential, and you will eventually push aside the dreams that you once had for yourself because you are not being inspired to do more by the company you keep.

However, if you surround yourself with individuals who you can learn from, who push you, and who motivate you, you can use what you have learned, apply it to your life, and consequently increase the likelihood of success in your own lane.

Similar to how the greatest basketball players on the face of the earth have facets of their game that need improvement, even the smartest or most successful person has an area of his or her life in which he or she has room to improve.

There is someone who does something better than you and, at the same time, there is something you do better than him or her. Having a relationship with that person can be mutually beneficial and prompt each of you to grow in some capacity you may not have otherwise grown without that interaction.

When you are the only go-getter out of all the people you interact with, sooner or later you are going to lower your standards for life and disregard your dreams. Eventually, you will begin to unconsciously sink to the level of complacency of those who are around you. You are better than that. You deserve the best that life has to offer. That includes the best people. It may be tough to cut off family, friends, and significant others who have been in your life for a long time but if they are not adding anything to your life, you have to make the decision for yourself to stop interacting with them. Only the people who encourage you to grow should be a part of your journey.

Some of the greatest players in NBA history have never won a championship. They may have great individual stats and perhaps hold some records, but because the pieces on their teams were not there, they always came up short in their quest to win a championship. In recent years, we've even seen superstars join teams with other superstars who could help them accomplish their goal of winning a championship. I'm not arguing for or against the decisions of these players, but rather using these examples to put things into perspective for you. If some of the top athletes in the world recognize they cannot win on their own and that their goal of winning a championship depends in part on the player make up of their team, what makes you think you can be successful with people in your life who do nothing but hold you back from realizing your greatness?

It may be necessary for you to make the unpopular decision to disassociate with a certain friend or a group of people so that you can begin building with those who will help you achieve your dreams. Best believe you're going to get criticized. People are going to say you think you're too good for them. If they are content with remaining stagnate, they're absolutely right—you are too good for them. If you want to elevate yourself, you have to elevate your associations.

Sometimes we outgrow people, for whatever reason. It is a part of life. Some people are around for a season and others are around for a lifetime. Learn to distinguish one from the other. Don't cling to people because of the length of time you have known them. Rather, maintain relationships based on the positive interactions you have with each other. It is okay to part ways when value is no longer added to your life with a particular association. Wish them well and pray for them, but move on.

It is also necessary to get rid of people who tell you everything you want to hear—better known as "yes men." Point blank, yes men (or yes people) can ruin your life because they often have hidden agendas. They are only concerned about your well-being *as long* as it involves some form of personal gain for them.

Instead of allowing yes people to occupy your space, keep those in your company who were there for you from the beginning and those who will hold you accountable for your actions. Those who will always tell you what you *need* to hear as opposed to what you want to hear. Cherish the people who would rather hurt your feelings momentarily by telling you the truth about yourself as a means to prevent long-term pain and suffering. Having people around who can provide you with constructive criticism is necessary if you want to take your life to the next level. Your ego and your pride may take a hit, but you have to realize that it is all for your benefit.

Always remember, the constructive criticism that your true friends provide you with is coming from a place of love, respect, and the genuine desire to see you become better. They may not always be right, but at least you know they are willing to disagree with you if they feel your actions conflict with your vision for a better life.

The individuals who are a part of my inner circle have no problem telling me about myself. They do it all the time, with no punches held. What they say may hurt at times but I don't take it personal because the constructive criticism they provide is for my benefit, as they only want me to be my best self.

Without accountability you will continue to do the same things over and over again that cause you to remain stagnant and potentially lead you down a destructive path. When no one is checking you or being honest with you, you are operating under the assumption that everything you do is right. Not one person on this earth is perfect. I don't know it all. You don't know it all. Thus, we can all benefit from the insight of others.

Just like it is necessary to take inventory of your thoughts, it is also necessary to take inventory of the people you surround yourself with. Those who encourage you, push you to do better, offer constructive criticism, and add value to your life are the only people you should be interacting with.

Elevation requires separation. On your path to achieving your goals, make the conscious decision to leave behind negativity, toxicity, and stagnation. Only surround yourself with people who can assist you on your journey and serve as positive reinforcement in the pursuit of your best life.

9

Overcome Adversity

No matter how far life pushes you down, no matter how much you hurt, you can always bounce back.
SHERYL SWOOPES
1st woman to be signed to the WNBA, 4-time WNBA Champion, 3-time WNBA MVP, 6-time WNBA All-Star, and a 2016 Naismith Basketball Hall of Fame inductee

In life, wrenches are going to be thrown our way. Something adverse is going to happen from time to time. Nevertheless, no matter what misfortunes may occur, it is up to us to rebound from them. It is up to us to bounce back from moments of adversity and continue on the path towards living our best lives.

When you experience moments of adversity, you haven't lost. Rather, tough times serve as opportunities for you to push through your present predicament and find a way to get past it. No obstacle is too great for you to overcome if what's on the other side of that obstacle is something that you truly want and will make your life better.

A family member may pass away unexpectedly, you and your significant other may end a long-term relationship or marriage, you may be diagnosed with an illness, you may get let go from your job, or your business may fail. Something is going to happen eventually. However, it is your duty to push through the adversity you face and to overcome it. This will make you stronger and more resilient, allowing you to be better prepared to handle any hardships that may come your way in the future.

Basketball players often go through situations that can have an adverse effect on their careers. Trades, injuries, getting benched, personal hardships. Many players are unable to bounce back from the adversity they've faced. At the same time, there are those who have continued to push through and play at a high level despite their circumstances or the occurrence of setbacks.

Isaiah Thomas lost his sister during the 2017 post-season. He scored 33 points the night after she passed and led the Boston Celtics to the Eastern Conference Finals.

New York Knicks legend Willis Reed who sat out of Game 6 of the 1970 NBA Finals due to a torn muscle in his thigh, played in Game 7 despite his injury to help the Knicks win the championship.

Alonzo Mourning retired from basketball in 2003 due to a kidney disease. After receiving a kidney transplant, Mourning returned to the NBA in 2004 and would win an NBA championship in 2006 with the Miami Heat.

Dwyane Wade overcame academic ineligibility during his freshman year at Marquette University, which sidelined him the entire season, to become the 5th pick in the 2003 NBA Draft, a 3-time NBA champion, and a 12-time All-Star.

There are countless stories of players who have overcome adversity to play at a high level. But one of the most well documented tales of overcoming adversity in the NBA is the journey of Golden State Warriors guard Shaun Livingston.

Shaun Livingston entered the NBA being heralded as one of the league's next superstars. He led his high school basketball team to two state championships, was named Illinois' "Mr. Basketball" and a McDonald's All-American during his senior year, and originally committed to attend Duke University before declaring for the NBA draft.

A 6'7 point guard, Livingston towered over other NBA point guards, yet was just as fast as the smaller guards in addition to having great court vision and passing ability. Analysts compared him to Los Angeles Lakers great Magic Johnson before he even suited up for an NBA game.[x] With the 4th pick in the 2004 NBA draft, the Los Angeles Clippers selected Livingston straight out of high school. Livingston's upside was tremendous. His potential was boundless. His game continued to develop and he kept getting better. Until what is considered one of the most horrific injuries in NBA history occurred.

On February 26, 2007, Livingston landed awkwardly after attempting a layup. He resultantly snapped his leg, injuring almost every major part of his left knee. He tore his ACL, MCL, PCL, and meniscus as well as dislocated his patella and tibiofibular joint. He was even told by one medical professional that he might have to get his leg amputated.[xi] Livingston missed the entire 2007-2008 NBA season in order to rehabilitate from his injury. When the season ended and Livingston's contract with the Clippers expired, the organization did not extend an offer to retain him, making him a free agent. About sixteen months after sustaining his injury, Livingston was permitted to return to basketball activities.

From the 2008-2009 season to the 2013-2014 season, Livingston had stints with 8 different NBA teams, an NBA Development League team, and was waived 4 different times. However, against all odds, Livingston was seemingly back to good form and in good health. He went on to have a breakout year in 2013-2014 with the Brooklyn Nets, starting in 76 games for the team.

In the summer of 2014, Livingston signed a $16.3 million deal to play with the Golden State Warriors and became a critical piece of the Warriors regular rotation during the 2014-2015 season, helping the team win the 2015 NBA championship. Livingston was also instrumental in helping the Warriors to a 73-9 regular season record in 2016—an NBA record. Lastly, he was once again a critical piece in helping the Warriors win back-to-back championships in 2017 and 2018.

What many do not know is that Livingston saw his path back to the NBA and regaining relevancy in the league as being tasks greater than himself. His purpose, in his own words, is to "inspire people to get through hard time and struggle." He wants people to use his story to "stand up, be strong willed and persevere."[xii]

Rough patches in life are inevitable. There will be times where you may feel like things can't get any worse.

You will feel like you want to give up. But if you are at your lowest point, feel somewhat encouraged—that means things can only get better. When you are at the bottom, the only thing left for you to do is to begin your ascent to the top. Never be content with conceding to adversity. No one has ever accomplished anything of great merit without enduring hard times and overcoming obstacles. With God on your side, you can get through anything.

When you recognize that the trajectory of your life is guided by Divine Influence, the setbacks, delays, and adverse situations that occur along the way to realizing your dreams will not seem that significant in the grand scheme of things. You will realize that everything happens for a reason—to put you in a better position for the future.

You are certainly capable of doing anything you put your mind to and accomplishing the goals you have set for yourself. However, that doesn't mean it will happen when and exactly how you want it to, and it certainly doesn't mean that you won't endure any trials along the way to accomplishing your goals.

You have two choices when adversity comes your way:

1) Mope around, feel sorry for yourself, and do nothing

or

2) Be proactive and change your circumstances through hard work and affirmative action.

The only alternatives are to either succumb or overcome. If you choose to succumb to your circumstances, you will never be able to realize the life you want for yourself. You will start a pattern of giving up when times get hard. However, if you choose to overcome your circumstances, you will be better equipped to face hard times in the future and be better prepared to accomplish the things in life you desire to accomplish. You are far stronger than any pain you may endure. For in painfully hard times there are lessons that teach us about ourselves.

Find the lessons in the journey. It is an amazing and encouraging feat alone, even when the chips are seemingly stacked against you, to continue to fight and push through. You will learn so much about who you are, what you are made of, and subsequently arm yourself with the tools to rise above anything unfavorable that comes your way.

The seemingly adverse positions you find yourself in are merely opportunities to grow—in faith and in effort. Be faithful knowing that the work you put in will eventually pay off, and if it doesn't go exactly the way you envisioned it would, trust that God's plan for you is perfect—and much better than you could ever fathom. Everything happens when and how it's supposed to happen. Whether you choose to acknowledge it or not, everything that happens to you can be used in your favor.

You cannot predict adversity. And you cannot rush greatness. What you can do is consistently work towards your goal and overcome obstacles along the way until you inevitably get to where you want to be.

FOURTH QUARTER

10
Hold That L

I've missed more than 9,000 shots in my career. I've lost almost 300 games. Twenty-six times, I've been trusted to take the game winning shot and missed. I've failed over and over and over again in my life. And that is why I succeed.
MICHAEL JORDAN
6-time NBA champion, 5-time NBA MVP, 14-time NBA All-Star, and a 2009 Naismith Basketball Hall of Fame inductee

Growing up, my twin brother and I used to have 1-on-1 wars. My grandfather built us a makeshift basketball court on a random 10 ft. by 10 ft. slab of concrete outside of his house. The "basket" was made of a long wooden pole from Home Depot, a random piece of plywood for a backboard, and a hoop purchased from Modell's Sporting Goods. Most of our adolescent summers were spent going at it on that slab of concrete.

When either of us lost, the loser automatically called for a rematch. No breaks, just "check it back up." We'd play all day and all night until it got dark or my mom told us it was time to go home or, more often than not, we ended up fighting. Whatever the reason was, neither of us could ever concede to losing. No way he or I was content going home holding an L (loss). The only thing that mattered was winning and being on top at the end of the day.

In retrospect, when he won more games in our daily series than me, I don't think I ever evaluated why I lost. I was only concerned with continually playing until I won. Not recognizing that if I actually reflected on what I did to influence the previous L and looked to correct those actions, I'd improve my chances of winning the next game. Instead, I'd just end up losing again.

This kind of behavior is still applicable in our lives as young and older adults. We fail in a certain capacity and instead of reflecting on the failure and making an attempt to learn from it, we typically just continue to do the same exact things we did before that got us to the unfavorable results.

There are valuable lessons provided in every L we take. Failure promotes growth. Failure teaches us what it takes to win, and to keep winning. Hence, failure can oftentimes be the best thing to ever happen to us. As long as we appreciate it for what it is—a learning opportunity.

Hold your L. Appreciate it. Instead of looking at failure as your own personal inability to do something, look at it solely as an opportunity to improve yourself and to learn from your previous missteps. Do not give up on yourself or your dreams because things did not go the way you anticipated they would on your first, second, or even third try. Rather, use those experiences to critically analyze what it was that you did ineffectively *then* take the necessary steps to correct that behavior. You will become better equipped to handle the challenges you encounter in the future.

If what you are seeking to accomplish is worthwhile and adds benefit to your life, then it is worth doing badly, *until* you get it right. Do not let inexperience or the prospect of failure discourage you. Do the work on yourself that is necessary to overcome the obstacles that you were previously hindered by.

Many times we refuse to accept our failures because of the ego. Naturally, we want to believe everything we are doing is right and the reason we have failed is not because of our own selves, but rather because of someone or something else's doing. We place the blame on external factors instead of taking ownership of our own stuff. "It can't be me" is one of the greatest lies ever told and comes directly from that little voice in our heads called the ego. In this life, you can either be a host to God, or a hostage to your ego. Not both. When you make the decision to become a host to God and swallow your pride, let go of your ego, accept your shortcomings, see failure as an opportunity to grow, and dedicate yourself to learning and improving, you will then see positive changes in your life.

There is always some facet of your life that you can improve upon, so through failure, you get a better idea of what to do and what not to do as you continue to pursue your goals. You learn what your strengths are as well as your weaknesses. Once you identify your strengths and weaknesses, you can then begin to work on improving in the areas you are not particularly strong in.

Failure is inevitable when you're attempting to do something extraordinary. Anyone who has ever done anything great has failed at some point. We were not put on this earth to merely subsist and try to "get by" or "just make it." We were put on this earth to be the greatest representations of ourselves and to get the most out of life that we possibly can.

Successful completion of a task should always be the goal. However, if you succeed at something 100% of the time and you never stumble, that may be an indication that you are not pushing yourself hard enough. When you play it safe, you are wasting away the God-given talents and opportunities you have been blessed with. Most times the tendency to play it safe is due to one's fear of failing. But what you have to understand is that failing is a part of life. There is no getting around it. You can try to avoid it at all costs and guess what? You will end up living a life far less than the one you want and the one you truly deserve. So be brave and take the necessary risks. Weather the storms of rejection, hurt, pain, and loss. Fail consistently, yet learn from your past experiences and previous approaches to a specific task. Keep fighting until you accomplish your goals.

Are you willing to look back on your life and be content with having a goal and wanting to accomplish it, yet you did not pursue it out of the fear of failing? Are you willing to live with yourself knowing that within you there is immense potential that is untapped and just lying dormant? With failure comes experience and growth. Embrace it. What you learn from the L's you take can serve as a catalyst for helping you get one step closer to attaining everything you want in life.

Failure is inevitable when you start doing something that is out of your comfort zone or when you pursue an endeavor you have no previous experience or knowledge in. However, it is failure that teaches you the valuable lessons you need to learn in order to get to that next level in life. Through failure you have been given the opportunity to learn and grow. Through learning and growing, comes maturation. When you know better, you do better. Only then will you be able to live the life you are destined to live.

Every basketball fan is pretty familiar with the dominance of Michael Jordan and the Chicago Bulls in the 1990s. Although the Bulls had a stranglehold on the NBA during that decade, what often goes overlooked, and under-appreciated, is the struggle the team endured on the road to winning their first NBA Championship. From 1988 to 1990, the Chicago Bulls were defeated in the playoffs by the eventual Eastern Conference Champions, and NBA Champions in 1989 and 1990—the Detroit Pistons.

Infamously known as "The Bad Boys" for their physically imposing, defense-oriented style of play, the Pistons employed a strategy against Michael Jordan known as "The Jordan Rules." The objective of the Jordan Rules was to essentially slow Jordan down offensively by being extra physical with him and forcing him to defer to his lesser talented teammates. Battling mental and physical fatigue,

The Bulls were unable to overcome the Piston's effective strategy and were eliminated from championship contention by the same team, three years in a row.

In 1991, the Bulls returned to the Eastern Conference Finals once again to face their nemesis, the Detroit Pistons. The team adopted a different offensive scheme this time known as the "triangle offense," they grew both physically and mentally stronger, Scottie Pippen emerged as a premier player in the league competing alongside Jordan, and other teammates stepped up their level of play as well.

As a result, the Bulls swept the Pistons in four games and defeated the Los Angeles Lakers in the 1991 NBA Finals to win the NBA championship. The Bulls would go on to win a total of 6 NBA Championships from 1991 to 1998. They won the league championship three consecutive years in a row, twice—from 1991 to 1993 and from 1996 to 1998.

Michael Jordan stated, "The team [Pistons] pushed us to a certain level. I don't think we would've won those six championships without getting over that hump in Detroit."[xiii] Coming up short numerous times against the Pistons prompted Jordan and the Bulls to learn what they needed to do in order to defeat their greatest adversary and helped them establish themselves as an NBA dynasty.

You can continue to do the same ineffective things over and over again. If you choose to do so, you should also expect the same results. But if you take the time to learn and grow from your missteps, you will be able to improve your approach to your goals and ultimately realize the life you want for yourself.

Failure teaches us a great deal about ourselves. It reveals our resiliency in the face of adversity and our ability to persevere when things do not necessarily go in our favor. James 1:4 (NIV) states, "Let perseverance finish its work, so that you may be mature and complete, not lacking anything." When you push through setbacks, you are arming yourself with the tools that will improve the likelihood of successfully completing your objectives in the long run.

Without trials, you are incapable of knowing what you are truly able to accomplish. You are unable to reflect on previous hardships and use them to push you through future experiences. If you were able to overcome failure once, you are able to do it again. And again. And again.

Use your failures as fuel. Channel those feelings you had during moments of your previous failures to push past whatever stands in the way of you living your best life. Learn to separate what you do, from who you are. You are not a failure, you just happened to momentarily fail. The beautiful thing about failing is that you have the opportunity to reinvent yourself, reevaluate the approach you take to attain your goal, and go at it again. There are no limits on the amount of times you can try to accomplish something. Therefore, do not stop working for what you want until you attain it.

11
Know When It's Time To Hang It Up

Knowing when to retire is difficult for any athlete or businessperson. You have to give up so much and start another life. But making that decision and sticking to it is one of the most rewarding decisions you will ever make in your life. I encourage people to look at this moment as starting a new season in a different game.

BILL RUSSELL
11-time NBA Champion, 15-time NBA MVP, 12-time NBA All-Star, and a 1975 Naismith Basketball Hall of Fame inductee

A question you are probably asking yourself right now after reading the title of this chapter and the opening quote is *How can you tell me to let go of something right after you just told me to overcome adversity, hold an L, and embrace failure?* Sounds backwards right? Trust me, it isn't.

Only when an endeavor has the potential to improve your life, should you continue to pursue it—even if you fail repeatedly at it. If what you are pursuing does nothing to add to your life, but instead only takes away from it, then it is necessary to let it go. Again, remain steadfast in pursuing the things that will bring you happiness and allow you to live your best life. However, let go of the things that are holding you back from the life you are meant to live.

As humans, we have a habit of remaining in or revisiting situations that no longer serve our best interest but instead bring us more pain than peace. We tend to cling to the things that are holding us back. It is in our nature to want what we want, when we want it. Even if those wants and desires fall outside of God's much better plan for us. Then we wonder why we can never get to the next phase of our lives. Find the courage to let go of the things you cannot change and leave behind that which no longer adds value to your life.

Whether "it" is a job, a romantic relationship, a friendship, an academic track, a sport, or any other endeavor, when something does not bring you joy nor do you see consistent improvement in that area—even after putting forth your best effort—then it is time for you to move on. Your sanity and your well-being are not worth sacrificing. The longer you stay in situations that do not bring you happiness, the more likely you are to block the blessings that are waiting for you on the other side of those situations.

Some NBA players go on to have long, illustrious careers. On the contrary, others have careers that are cut short for a variety of different reasons but mainly due to injuries. When players have nothing else left in the tank to give, when they become mentally, physically, and emotionally fatigued with the grind of the NBA season, when their bodies are no longer able to recover from injuries, or when they realize they have accomplished everything they wanted to during their careers, they then make the conscious decision to retire and move on with their lives. It is a part of the game.

Probably one of the most noteworthy examples one can use to illustrate this principle is Brandon Roy.

Brandon Roy was selected with the 6th pick in the 2006 NBA Draft and was acquired by the Portland Trail Blazers on draft day via a trade. His impact in Portland was immediate. Roy was selected as the Rookie of the Year in his first NBA season, was a reserve on the Western Conference All-Star team in his second season, earned another All-Star selection while placing 9th in MVP voting in his third season, and, at the start of his fourth NBA season, signed a 5-year, max contract. Roy was poised to be an NBA superstar for many years to come. Unfortunately, his playing career was cut short.

Brandon Roy had been battling chronic knee problems since college and in December 2011, he announced his retirement from basketball. His knees had degenerated so much that he lacked cartilage between the bones in both of his knees. The face of the Trail Blazers franchise who seemed destined to go down as one of the league's greatest players and whom Kobe Bryant deemed as having "no weaknesses in his game,"[xiv] was leaving the game at the age of 27 and after only five seasons in the NBA.

Roy did attempt a comeback in 2012, but he only played in 5 games before having season-ending, and ultimately career-ending, surgery on his right knee. After the season ended, he stated (in reference to retiring), "It's never going to be easy, but it's a little smoother knowing I gave it a try and now it's time to move on."[xv]

In 2016, Roy became the head coach of Nathan Hale High School in his hometown of Seattle, Washington. He led the team to a 29-0 regular season record and was named the *Naismith National High School Coach of the Year*—a tremendous honor for any coach, let alone a first-year head coach. Even though the need to retire from playing was hard for him, Roy found another way to have an impact on the court—in the form of coaching and working with youth.

At some point, we are all going to have to retire from situations that no longer accurately represent who we are and who we aspire to be. The longer you stay in a situation that stagnates you, the more likely you are to block the blessings that God has in store for you.

If you are unhappy, walk away. Leave. If you have given everything you have to someone or something and your efforts are unappreciated or unproductive, at that point you need to throw in the towel and pursue what it is that will bring your life joy and peace.

Easier said than done, right? Trust me, I know all about that, as you will soon find out. It's tough to let go. Especially when we have become accustomed to and comfortable with the way things are. However, when you do walk away from something that no longer accurately reflects the person you want to be, you will gain a restored sense of self. A burden that has been weighing you down for so long will be lifted off of you and you will be able to exist in a space that brings you joy and peace. And, as a result, that which you truly want and will make you happy has no choice other than to show up in your life.

Back in 2011, I enrolled in a doctoral (PhD) program because I had a goal of getting the most formal education I could possibly attain in my field of study in addition to wanting to become a university professor.

Yeah, right. That's a bold face lie.

I enrolled in the doctoral program solely because even after receiving my master's degree that year, employers in my field still would not hire me. So, in order to further improve the likelihood of getting a job in my field (and to keep receiving a couple dollars per year for being a teacher's assistant), I enrolled in the PhD program to become more attractive to prospective employers.

At the beginning of the second year of my doctoral program, I was extended a job offer in my field of study. But even after I began working for my new employer, I remained in the program. Part of me did not want to abandon something that I started. I didn't want to be a quitter. Another part of me did not want to let down my family, advisors, friends, and those who looked up to me. I wanted to make other people proud. However, none of those reasons had anything to do with my own genuine desire to complete the program.

I completed my main objective (to get a job), yet because I refused to let go, I suffered internally and was unhappy for years. I was putting time, energy, and money into something I didn't believe added any additional value to my life and that did not line up with my long-term plans. As a result, I was neglecting the things that I really wanted to do and that would be fulfilling.

Finally, after 6 years of going back and forth and in and out of the program, I exited the doctoral program for good. It proved to be one of the best decisions that I have ever made in my life. I was now able to put my time, energy, and money into my passions. I expanded the reach and scope of my nonprofit organization's mentoring program. I started the 'Shoot Your Shot' blog. And I was able to put in the necessary time and effort to complete this book. Had I unhappily remained in the program, I would not have been able to do those things. My life is much better off after making the decision to let go of something that did not bring me happiness and that did not align with what I wanted to do with my life.

Be cognizant of when it is time to relinquish control, to let go, and to just leave it in God's hands. Don't waste away years of your life clinging to something that no longer fully represents you. Lean on your faith, knowing that God will not forsake you and that something greater is in store for you.

In your time of angst and uncertainty, what you need will be supplied to you. Separate yourself from anything that no longer allows you to be the best version of yourself. Only then can you begin to see the things appear in your life that will truly make you happy.

It's difficult to give up. Especially because we've been taught since we were young to "never give up." But if something no longer brings you happiness, or it causes you continual pain, and you've done the work to make things better to no avail, you have to let it go and move on.

Don't lose everything, chasing nothing. Don't block your blessings clinging to the past or to the things that do not bring any value to your life. If you continue to hold on to what could have been, you fail to open yourself up to what could be.

12
Your Health Is Your Wealth

Health is the most critical thing in our life. With your health anything is possible, without it you can't do anything.
BILL WALTON
2-time NBA champion, 1978 NBA MVP, 2-time NBA All-Star, and a 1993 Naismith Basketball Hall of Fame inductee

Professional athletes have an expectation by their team's front office, their coaches, their teammates, their agents, and their fan base that when they come into training camp before the regular season starts they are in shape and in good health. Being healthy and in shape prior to the start of the season are critical to players' success because they have to be ready for the adverse effect that the grind of the regular season and possibly the playoffs will have on their bodies.

Unfortunately, some players come back from their summer vacations out of shape and heavier than their normal playing weight. They did not mind their health or what they were eating and are, hence, more susceptible to the prospect of injury because they are pushing their body to a point that it cannot withstand.

In the basketball profession, a player's livelihood is dependent upon their health. By not being in good health, athletes are unable to perform at a high level and their inability to perform can result in them being benched, traded, or even cut from a team.

All of the principles and examples explored in the previous sections of this book can be utilized to help you accomplish your goals and live the life you've always envisioned. However, if you do not take care of yourself mentally, physically, spiritually and emotionally, all of the insight you have gained from this book will be for naught. What you have absorbed and intend on applying to your life will mean absolutely nothing if you are not in good health. Think about it, how can you do the things you need to do in order to live a better life if you are not in a healthy space to effectively do so? You cannot. Maintaining good health is a critical factor in getting what you want out of life.

When you take care of yourself, you physically feel good and have a positive perception of yourself. You have a more optimistic outlook on life. You have more energy. You perform more effectively. You are motivated to complete the tasks that are critical to accomplishing your goals.

On the other hand, if you are in poor health, you may not have the strength, energy, or motivation to perform those tasks that are critical to the accomplishment of your goals. You cannot live your best life if you are tired, run down, maligned with illness, or unable to do anything constructive because of your physical standing. No person can do what is necessary to attain success or enjoy the fruits of their labor without being in good health.

Being healthy is not solely based on how you look. You can be thin, "big boned," or muscular, and be healthy. You can also be unhealthy with those physical attributes. How you look is not the only determinant of your level of health.

As a society, we have begun to equate health and wellness with how one looks externally. And although one's outward appearance may be an indication of whether or not a person is living a healthy lifestyle, appearance is not the end all be all.

You can consume toxic products, try extreme diets and weight loss plans, and even get procedures done just to look fit or appear to be in great shape. However, those methods are not necessarily healthy and will possibly be at the expense of your long-term health and well-being. That is not maintaining a healthy lifestyle.

Maintaining a healthy lifestyle means being conscious of what you consume. It means staying active and exercising. It means drinking more water than you drink soda or juice. It means eating more vegetables than you eat junk food. You don't have to be a bodybuilder or a vegan to be healthy but what you cannot be is sedentary and consume filth on a regular basis.

In a November 2017 *Bleacher Report* article, NBA stars such as Kyrie Irving and Damian Lillard, in addition to a host of other NBA players, were profiled to shine a spotlight on their change in diet. The players adopted a plant based-diet and made the choice to eliminate meat from their eating regimen. Although one would think that professional athletes would have a hard time adhering to a vegetarian or vegan lifestyle, primarily because they are on the road all the time and expend so much energy on the court, seemingly needing animal protein, the contrary is true. Their decision to "eat cleaner" has actually had a positive impact on not only their on-court performance but also, more importantly, how their bodies felt overall. The players featured in the article who have adopted vegetarian or vegan lifestyles reported having more energy, quicker recovery, and more restful sleep since giving up animal products for meals.[xvi]

By no means am I trying to convince you to become a vegetarian or vegan. I personally tried a vegetarian lifestyle for a few months and it just didn't work out for me, namely because of the degree to which I travel. Would it work for you? Maybe, maybe not. That's for you to determine. Some of you may prefer to eat meat. Some of you may not. What works for you works for you. The point I am trying to make when it comes to your eating is to be more conscious and selective of what you put into your body. You are what you eat and that is reflective in not only your appearance but also in your performance and your overall health.

Make the necessary adjustments to your eating habits and eliminate products that potentially have an adverse effect on your long-term health. Find the balance that works for you. Regardless of how many days you are in the gym, you cannot outwork a bad diet. Eat in moderation, only up until the point that you are content. Be disciplined. Treat your body with respect and love. Treat it like it's the only one you get. Because, well, it is the only one you're going to get.

Your health is also not solely dependent on what you eat, how much you weigh, or how often you exercise either. It also depends on your mental, emotional, and spiritual standing.

Do you struggle with anxiety or depression? Are you in an unhealthy, abusive, or dead-end relationship that is causing you to engage in destructive behavior? Are you going through something that is testing your faith in a higher power? Do some serious introspection. If you do not do regular inventory on yourself or your surroundings, you risk getting lost in negativity that can adversely affect your health. If your health is in jeopardy, so is your livelihood.

Whatever is jeopardizing your well-being needs to first be addressed and then eliminated from your life immediately. Choose life. Choose to feel good about yourself and optimistic about the prospects of your future. Do not let anything or anyone compromise your well-being. You only have one life to live, so make it as stress-free, rewarding, and abundant as possible. The only way to do that is to make sure you are healthy in all areas of your life. No one can take care of you, better than you. So do not neglect your own livelihood. What you eat, the information you consume, the people you interact with, all have an impact on your health. Rid your life of the things that adversely affect your mental, emotional, spiritual, and physical health. Your health is paramount to living a fulfilled life.

One of my favorite commercials of all-time is the GEICO auto insurance commercial that featured NBA Hall of Famer and shot-blocking extraordinaire Dikembe Mutombo. In the commercial, a 7'2 Mutombo runs around to different places with the sole intent to deny men, women, and children from shooting different objects into their respective makeshift basketball hoops.

What took the commercial to the next level of hilarity for me was that after blocking the objects, Mutombo would smile, wave his index finger from side to side, declare "no, no, no," "not in my house," or "not today," laugh obnoxiously, and then run off to claim his next victim. (I'm going somewhere with this, I promise.)

With the same enthusiasm that Dikembe Mutombo protected those makeshift basketball hoops in the commercial, protect your own peace in a similar manner. (See, I told you I was going somewhere.) Keep that same energy. Reject, any and everything—things, endeavors, and people alike—that has the potential to adversely affect your health (mental, spiritual, emotional, and physical), your mood, your productivity, your outlook on life, your interactions, and how you perceive yourself.

One of our primary duties in life is to fend off negativity and to avoid bad energy. Scripture says, do not be overcome by evil, but overcome evil with good. The first step in changing your own life and potentially the lives of others, is being at peace with yourself. Protect your peace. Your life, and the lives of those around you, depends on it.

You may be in a space where it's necessary to talk to someone about all that is going on in your life. If what you have done on your own in regards to personal maintenance up to this point in your life has not helped you to improve your well-being, then seek out someone who can help you in a way that you have not been able to help yourself thus far. Stop living in the personal prison you have put yourself in, in order to save face for others who have no idea of the struggles that you have been dealing with.

There is nothing wrong with being vulnerable with another party and discussing the issues you are having in your life with them. It is misguided, however, if you do not seek out the help that you need. You cannot heal what you never reveal. Whether you talk to a significant other, family member, close friend, pastor, or a therapist, there is someone who can help you.

There is no weakness in admitting you are going through something and that you need help to get past it. Admitting you are not able to do something on your own exudes strength and courage. Only if you are in a good space and are in good health will you be able to live the life you have envisioned for yourself.

Take ownership over your life. Make the decision that nothing is more important than your physical, mental, spiritual, and emotional well-being. That may sound selfish, but it is not. It is actually self-less. Taking care of yourself is the ultimate exercise of love. You can be of no benefit to anyone else if you are not in good health or do not have a positive perception of yourself.

Put your well-being first. Minding your health is, and should be, a daily exercise. So take the necessary steps to become healthy, in all areas of your life. Work out. Eat consciously. Rid yourself of negative influences. Meditate. Pray. Speak and think positively about yourself. Find an outlet to talk to. Be well on all fronts. And in all areas of your life. The groundwork for living your best life is having and sustaining good health.

END OF REGULATION

Second Half Highlights

The game isn't over just yet! We have a brief "Overtime" period coming up shortly but before we get to that, here are the "highlights" from the 2nd half of the book.

Success Leaves Clues

- At some point in time, someone has accomplished a goal similar to the one you aspire to accomplish. Study them.
- Mentorship is one of the greatest tools for success. Whatever avenue is available to you, actively seek guidance from those who are where you want to be.
- There is always something you can learn from someone else that will put you in a better position to be successful in your endeavors.

Your Dream Is Only As Good As Your Team

- Be selective of your interactions and whom you choose to spend your time with. Who you associate with has a profound impact on the direction your life goes in.

- Align yourself with people who you can learn from and who push you beyond your circumstances. If you want to elevate yourself, elevate your associations.

- Surround yourself with people who have the same degree of aspirations for their lives as you do, who encourage you to become the best version of yourself, and who want to see you live your best life.

Overcome Adversity

- Everything that happens in your life can be used to your advantage. The adverse positions you find yourself in are merely opportunities for you to grow.

- No one has ever accomplished anything great without enduring hard times and overcoming obstacles. You are in good company.

- Pushing past adversity makes you more resilient and prepares you to effectively handle hardship in the future.

Hold That L

- Failure promotes growth and teaches us what it takes to win. Embrace the L.

- Failure is inevitable when you do something for the first time and when you step out of your comfort zone. Succeeding 100% of the time is indication you are not pushing yourself hard enough.

- When you know better, you do better. Through failure, you learn and grow. When you learn and grow, you mature.

Know When It's Time To Hang It Up

- Let go of the things you cannot change and that which no longer adds value to your life.

- The longer you stay in situations that no longer bring you happiness, the more likely you are to block the blessings that God has in store for you. By holding on to what could've been, you fail to open yourself up to what could be.

- When you walk away from something that no longer accurately represents the person you want to be, that which will make you happy has no other choice than to show up in your life.

Your Health Is Your Wealth

- Maintaining good health is a critical factor in getting what you want out of life.
- Your health is not solely dependent on what you eat or how you look but also depends on your mental, emotional, and spiritual standing. If your health is in jeopardy, so is your livelihood.
- Taking care of yourself is the ultimate expression of love and a necessary daily exercise. No one can take better care of you than you.

OVERTIME

13
Maintain An Attitude Of Gratitude

If we magnified blessings as much as we magnified disappointments, we would all be much happier.
JOHN R. WOODEN
10-time NCAA men's basketball champion as coach, 5-time Associated Press College Coach of the Year, and a 2-time (as a player and coach) Naismith Basketball Hall of Fame inductee

When professional athletes win awards and championships, or receive contract extensions and endorsement deals, something that the majority of them do is give thanks. In 2014, Kevin Durant won the NBA's Most Valuable Player Award. During his acceptance speech, Durant thanked God, his teammates, coaches, family members, and organizational staff, among others.

Most notably, it was when Durant deemed his mother "The Real MVP" that he was unofficially inducted into the social media hall of fame. But something got lost in the meme-mania and hashtag-craze surrounding Durant's emotional tribute to his mother: his genuine display of gratitude.

Even though it was solely Durant's performance on the court that earned him the MVP honor, he acknowledged that without the role others played in his life, he would not be standing at that podium accepting the award.

The importance of being grateful for what we have, how far we have come, and the help that we have received along the way is often overlooked. Which makes sense; we live in a society where a person can never have enough of anything. We take what we have for granted. We focus on what we do not have and covet what others have instead of appreciating the things already in our possession.

Maintaining an attitude of gratitude is key if you want to live the life you've always envisioned for yourself. By genuinely being grateful for what you have, you are preparing yourself for the abundance of blessings that are destined to come your way.

For gratitude draws you closer to the source from which all blessings flow—God.

Be thankful for the job you have that may not necessarily be the one you want, but it pays the bills. Be thankful for the roof over your head even if you desire a bigger and better space. Be thankful for the clean clothes on your back and the reliable shoes on your feet even if they aren't popular name brands. Be thankful for the food you eat. For your friends, family, and loved ones. For being blessed with another day of life. Et cetera, et cetera, et cetera. You cannot have an expectation to receive more if you are not appreciative for what you already have. The two just don't go together.

On a daily basis, I reflect on my life and what I am thankful for. I either write down in a journal what I am grateful for or I silently thank God for the multitude of things and people that I have been blessed with.

I also make it a priority to take time during my day (especially during times of high stress or discouragement) to just be still and reflect again on the blessings in my life. Before I go to bed, I reflect back on my day, highlighting the positive events that took place and the tasks I was able to successfully complete.

By doing this, I am constantly reminded of how blessed I am. Regularly acknowledging my blessings puts me in a better space for the current day and the following day, as I am making the conscious decision to focus on the positive aspects of my life.

Even when I was at my lowest point in life (literally at my lowest because I was living underground in a basement apartment), I still made it a priority to reflect on the things that I had been blessed with and to do affirmations. I had a job to go to. I had a great support system that helped me in my times of need. I was living on my own and actively pursuing my dreams. Before I could ever fix my mouth up to complain about my circumstances or what I didn't have, there was so much more I had to be thankful for.

It does not matter if things are going well for you or you feel like they are going bad. Regardless of your circumstances, you have so many things to be thankful for. So, in every situation you find yourself in, give thanks.

Besides, focusing on what you do not have is counterproductive. When you do so, you are essentially projecting negative energy. When you are not thankful for what you have, you are, in turn, focusing on a lack thereof of certain things. What you focus on manifests and multiplies. When you focus on lack, you attract more lack into your life. Yet, when you focus on your blessings, you attract more blessings into your life.

There is nothing wrong with continually setting higher goals for yourself and trying to accomplish more with your life. You should aspire to reach a higher level in your career, earn multiple degrees, pursue your passion, or start a business. God requires us to strive to be the best versions of ourselves. However, you can aspire to be greater than you currently are, while being thankful for what you have presently. Being thankful despite your circumstances not only affects you, but can also serve as encouragement for others to be thankful for all the things they have in their lives.

Those around you, personally or professionally, will look at your consistent attitude of gratitude and see that despite your circumstances, you are still thankful for what you currently have. Good vibes rub off. As do positive and assertive actions. You can be the inspiration behind your counterparts' applying an attitude of gratitude in their own lives.

Lead by example in all that you do. Including being thankful. By continually holding a position of gratitude, you are serving as an example to others to be thankful for all the things they have in their lives and to recognize they are blessed and better off than most. The example you are setting will help others change their lives for the better.

What you currently have and where you currently are in life essentially prepares you for what will soon come. Even if you aspire to achieve more, be thankful for what you already have. You can either focus on what you do have or what you do not have. Whichever option you choose to focus on, will multiply. So choose wisely.

When you lead with a grateful heart and focus on the positive aspects of your life, you are establishing a closer relationship with God. A closer connection with God allows us to be more in tune with the creative powers within us. With a stronger realization of our creative powers, we are able to manifest into our lives whatever it is that we want.

14

Pay It Forward

Giving back to the community is where my heart is so if I can help even a couple of people then I'm doing my job. I'm blessed to be able to do this work.
CARMELO ANTHONY
10-time NBA All-Star

NBA Cares is the league's platform for addressing social issues and provides the opportunity for teams and players to be involved in the global community through service and advocacy. It is a requirement for every player in the NBA to participate in community service outreach events. At the same time, there are players who go above and beyond to serve their communities and give back outside of their requirement as employees of the National Basketball Association.

Many NBA players have started their own foundations or have partnered up with local and national organizations that address issues they are interested in. For instance, in 2016 Chris Paul was named ESPN's Sports Humanitarian of the Year for his work in the community. The Chris Paul Family Foundation serves and provides resources to underprivileged communities. He and the foundation have pledged over $1 million to Boys & Girls Clubs across the country. He established a scholarship fund to students at Wake Forest University—his undergraduate institution. Paul hosts a variety of yearly fundraising events to raise money to provide children with resources that can assist them in succeeding in life. He has also made it a priority to build computer labs and place updated technology in underprivileged schools across the country.

As an extension of his foundation and in partnership with Akron Public Schools, LeBron James opened the I Promise School on July 30, 2018. The school serves at-risk children in Akron, Ohio with a focus on accelerated learning in order to bring kids up to speed who otherwise might be lagging and on combating factors outside the classroom that could cause children to struggle. Through the LeBron James Family Foundation, James has also pledged to pay for more than 1,000 kids to attend college. Students who complete the I Promise School's program will get tuition paid for by James to the University of Akron beginning in 2021.

Many other former and current players in the league have causes of their own or work with other organizations addressing issues that resonate with them including Jalen Rose, Carmelo Anthony, Russell Westbrook, Joakim Noah, Derrick Rose, Kevin Durant, Luol Deng, and Pau Gasol, among numerous others. While their job is to play basketball, these players understand that their purpose is much bigger than solely performing on the court. They recognize they are in a position to help others succeed, hence they dedicate their time, energy, resources, money, and voice to initiatives that help others who are in need. They have used their platform to reach back and make an impact.

The accumulation of material possessions is the by-product of you finding yourself, putting in the necessary work, and having faith that what you want is coming to you. When you go throughout life operating in purpose, abundance has no choice but to be attracted to you. As we just discussed, for all that we receive, we should maintain an attitude of gratitude.

The act of giving is a socially responsible expression of gratitude. Through giving, we are communicating to God that we are thankful for all the blessings we have received, and grateful to be in a position to help others in their time of need. Giving is a means for us to show our appreciation for our standing in life.

You don't have to break the bank or give what you don't have. Giving back does not always have to be monetary. You can give back through your time, your words, and your actions. You can mentor students. You can speak to youth groups. You can volunteer at shelters and community centers. You can coach sports teams. You can donate old clothing or canned goods. You can refer people to job opportunities.

2 Corinthians 9:12 (NIV) states, "Each of you should give what you have decided in your heart to give, not reluctantly or under compulsion, for God loves a cheerful giver. And God is able to bless you abundantly, so that in all things at all times, having all that you need, you will abound in every work." When you receive, give. And when you give, you will be blessed with more.

One of the most fulfilling experiences a person can ever have is helping others. When we give, we are essentially communicating to God and ourselves that we have more than enough. You will not only feel as though you are living in abundance, but you will also feel better about yourself for assisting others. Through giving, you are also acknowledging your duty to mankind and fulfilling your social obligation to help others when they need it most. We have been blessed in so many ways that we often overlook our blessings on a daily basis. And we often try to hold on to what we have out of fear that we may lose it. That which you cling to, you will eventually lose. You cannot take anything with you when you die, so why hold on to it when there is someone out there who could use what you have?

Be a blessing to others. If you sow sparingly, you reap sparingly. But if you sow generously, you reap generously. Not only does giving provide a boost to your own moral, but it also boosts the moral of those you are helping. Your actions may even inspire those who you have helped and motivate them to give back when they are in a position to do so.

Once you get into the habit of contributing to the well-being and the betterment of others, the quality of your own life will continually increase. Through giving, we are pleasing God and positioning ourselves to be receptive to more blessings.

POSTGAME

The "game" is over, now what? Well, now the real work begins. It's always easy to apply the things that we've learned while we are working our way through a book or immediately after we've finished it. The hard part is to keep applying what we've learned after some time has passed so that we do not start reverting back to our old habits.

With that being said, I charge you to make the commitment to do something every day—starting right now—that sets in motion the process of you attaining the life you aspire to live. It can be as simple as sending an email, making a phone call, or looking up information about an endeavor. Paraphrasing slightly what the guy from those old Everest College commercials used to say, "Why don't you [do something today] that's going to help you in your future?" Shoot your shot and keep shooting it. Continue to build upon your initial efforts day after day until you get to where you want to be.

If you enjoyed *Shoot Your Shot* and you took something of value from it, I ask of you to do me two HUGE favors: 1) Please rate the book and write a review for it on Amazon.com *and* 2) Please refer this book to your network, your family members, your friends, your teammates, your colleagues, and your social media following—pretty much everyone you know.

Reviews and referrals are the primary means that word about this book will spread, resulting in it reaching as many people as possible—which is the goal. Your support in this way is much needed in order for this book to have its' intended impact. I've said it before and I'll say it again, I really appreciate you for taking the time to read this book. Thank you, from the bottom of my heart.

Acknowledgements

First, and foremost, I would like to thank God, the Source of all of my blessings. Thank you Lord for assigning me this task and for giving me the strength, wisdom, and fervor to finish this book.

Courteney—thank you for your love, patience, understanding, and continual support during the long process of completing this book, as well as with all of the other endeavors I pursue. You are amazing and your support is everything. I love you and I am eternally grateful to the Lord for bringing you into my life.

To my mother—thank you for putting the pen in my hand, for making me read when I didn't want to, and for stressing the importance of embracing my creativity and individuality. This would not be possible had it not been for all the sacrifices you made and for the lessons you have taught me. I love you.

Terrell, Michelle, Kaiesha, Umar, Ryan, Steve, Marcus, Karyn, Lonnie, Nate, Vic, Jared, Darrel, Jeff, Mike, Mitch—thank you for being a part of my "Team." I appreciate you all for always having my back, for supporting me, for believing in me, for speaking life into me, and for helping me to become the man I am today. I couldn't ask for a better squad.

Coach Thompson, Uncle Ed, Uncle Steve, Mr. Shawn, Ms. Jackie (RIP), Dr. Jozefowicz, Dr. Asamoah, Dr. Walford—thank you for taking on the task of serving as my mentors and for seeing something in me that I couldn't yet see in myself. Thank you for believing in me and for investing in me. Your advocacy and your support mean the world.

Emy—thank you for all of your feedback, resources, and encouragement during this process and for helping me step-by-step through this book. I am truly appreciative for everything you have done.

Family, extended family, friends, and loved ones—thank you for all of your words of encouragement, your prayers, and your continual support.

And last, but certainly not least, thank YOU, the reader, for supporting me by purchasing and reading this book. Words cannot express how grateful I am to you for seeing value in this work. You are the reason for this book. I truly hope you are able to take something from this book that will help you in your personal walk. Thank you.

About The Author

An emerging voice for the millennial generation, VERNON BRUNDAGE JR. uses fresh and innovative approaches to inspire and motivate others to become their greatest selves.

Receiving formal training in the economics discipline, Vernon is currently employed as an Economist for the United States federal government. He is also the founder and Executive Director of *investED* Enrichment Services, Inc., a 501(c)(3) non-profit organization that serves at-risk youth in low-income communities. Additionally, Vernon is a youth and young adult speaker as well as the founder and principle writer of the 'Shoot Your Shot' blog.

Vernon hails from the Philadelphia, Pennsylvania region and currently resides in the Washington, DC metropolitan area. For more information about Vernon, visit vernonbrundage.com.

References

[i] Barron, D. (2013). *Lin tells "60 Minutes" his ethnicity*

[ii] *60 Minutes.* "Giannis Antetokounmpo, the Milwaukee Bucks' 'Greek Freak." Corresponded by Steve Kroft. CBS News. March 27, 2018.

[iii] Pollakoff, B. (2013). *Gregg Popovich says Bruce Bowen 'couldn't dribble and couldn't pass.'* Accessed November 8, 2017 through https://nba.nbcsports.com/2013/11/02/gregg-popovich-says-bruce-bowen-couldnt-dribble-and-couldnt-pass/

[iv] Haefner, J. (2008). *Mental Rehearsal & Visualization: The Secret to Improving Your Game Without Touching a Basketball!* Accessed February 23, 2017 through https://www.breakthroughbasketball.com/mental/visualizatio n.html

[v] Coelho, P. *The Alchemist.* 1993. New York, NY: Harper-Collins.

[vi] MacMullan, J. (2016). *Kobe's final hour: How advice from the King of Pop shaped one of the NBA's most legendary careers.* Accessed May 12, 2018 through http://www.espn.com/nba/story/_/id/15193525/kobe-bryant-personal-mount-rushmore-mentors-starring-michael-jackson

[vii] ESPN.com. (2009). *The Calculus of a Crossover.* Accessed April 13, 2018 through

http://www.espn.com/blog/truehoop/post/_/id/5645/the-calculus-of-a-crossover

viii Garcia, Bobbito. (2016). *The Legend of Pearl*. Accessed April 22, 2018 through https://www.slamonline.com/streetball/the-legend-of-pearl-washington/

ix Jenkins, L. (2017). *The Beard: James Harden Untangles His Life And Game.* Accessed July 20, 2018 through https://www.si.com/nba/2017/02/28/james-harden-the-beard-houston-rockets-mike-dantoni

x Abrams, J. (2013). *Like Magic.* Accessed January 5, 2018 through http://grantland.com/features/on-career-shaun-livingston-survived-one-worst-injuries-nba-history/

xi Abrams, J. (2013). *Like Magic.* Accessed January 5, 2018 through http://grantland.com/features/on-career-shaun-livingston-survived-one-worst-injuries-nba-history/

xii Spears, M. (2016). *Can't Be Defeated: The Shaun Livingston Story*. Accessed January 5, 2018 through https://theundefeated.com/features/never-defeated-the-shaun-livingston-story/

xiii *ESPN Films 30 for 30.* "Bad Boys." Directed by Zak Levitt. Written by Aaron Cohen and Zak Levitt. ESPN Films. April 17, 2014.

xiv Nelson, R. (2010). *Kobe Bryant: Roy over Durant.* Accessed October 22, 2017 through

http://www.slamonline.com/nba/kobe-bryant-roy-over-durant/#ScDtzhH6gwzjFmhf.97

xv Pelton, K. (2013). *Brandon Roy calls it a career*. Accessed on October 22, 2017 through http://www.espn.com/blog/truehoop/post/_/id/60185/brandon-roy-calls-career

xvi Haberstroh, T. (2017). *The Secret (But Healthy!) Diet Powering Kyrie And The NBA*. Accessed December 22, 2017 through https://bleacherreport.com/articles/2744130-the-secret-but-healthy-diet-powering-kyrie-and-the-nba